A Reporter Finds God

Through Spiritual Healing

by

EMILY GARDINER NEAL

MOREHOUSE-BARLOW CO.

NEW YORK

PRINTED IN THE UNITED STATES OF AMERICA

BY THE HADDON CRAFTSMEN, INC., SCRANTON, PA.

To my husband
Alvin Willard Neal

Foreword

THE MYSTERY of pain and suffering, of healing and health has always haunted mankind. The very young ask questions that the very learned stutter with uncertainty in answering. Man has lavished recklessly his energy in seeking the solution.

God, no doubt, wills it so. As George Herbert once wrote:

> "...................that at last,
> If goodness lead him not, yet weariness
> May toss him to my breast."

When an eager, competent, and fair mind wrestles with this mystery, the struggle is not only worth reading about, but the outcome can be exciting.

Emily Gardiner Neal certainly was eager to get at the heart of the mystery and show up those whose answers were hopelessly superstitious and medieval. She brought the skeptic's prejudice, but she was fair-minded. And she was honest, fearlessly honest.

I first met her after the weekly services of healing which I conducted in my parish in Pittsburgh. Bishop Pardue, I believe, had told her about the services. She came up to me, bright-eyed with questions and ruthless in her cross-examination. She believed nothing and dissected everything.

As time went on we became close friends and in friendly fashion indulged in lengthy debates. One could call them arguments. She also worshipped regularly on weekdays as well as on Sunday. Names of her family were added to our prayer list. No one fought the tendency "to go overboard" more fiercely than she did. Against the witness of her eyes and the experience of her heart, she placed the integrity and objectivity of a reporter. She must have the facts and the proof, and more proof, and documented proof.

The day came, as it almost always does to those who are fair-minded and honest, when the leap of faith was made. There could be no more denial of our Lord and the power of the Holy Spirit.

What began as a reporter's research into the phenomenon of so-called "spiritual" healing and the mystery of pain has now ended in a carefully recorded case history of a journey into faith.

Even as I received her typed manuscript I learned that her husband had been rushed to the hospital with a coronary illness. She attached a hasty note: "Pray hard for Alvin. I believe; therefore I am not panicky." Yes, she believes, and her faith has outstripped that of many of us who are ordained church workers.

How earnestly I long for all of the Church to recapture the fiery faith of the first Disciples. Here and there this faith is beginning to warm some hearts. Indeed, many daily are catching fire. Our author is one. Did not our Lord command us to heal in His name and to cast out devils which seek to distort and destroy the soul? How then can we affirm His Lordship and refuse to obey His most explicit command? One cannot arbitrarily decide which of our Lord's commands are commands and which can be ignored. One cannot accept forgiveness of one's sins, pronounced by the priesthood and mediated through the Church, and then reject the power of the Church to renew a right spirit and to make one whole again, physically and outwardly as well as spiritually and inwardly.

Mrs. Neal succinctly phrases much of our religious dilemma: "Fastening our eyes too intently on the Cross, we may become blind to the Resurrection." Often we emphasize man's sin and depravity and too seldom appreciate man's redemption and wholeness.

Is not the central fact of the Gospel the Good News that Jesus Christ, God made flesh, came to earth not to condemn and destroy humanity, but to transform people into a new humanity, into new creatures?

For spiritual healing is but another way of saying spiritual wholeness. The wholeness or holiness of the spirit is irrevocably associated with physical healing and well-being. Man is both spirit and body. A Christian seeks to renew a right spirit within himself, that he might draw nearer to God through Christ. He loses himself that he might find himself; he dies to the old self that he might live a new creature. In brief, by repentance, by self-examination, by discipline, he wills to will the will of God. It is in such seeking that he finds, in losing that he is saved, in dying that he lives.

From such a rebirth bodies are physically healed. The healing is not sought for its own sake, but as a corollary. It is a gift, not a prize to be won. One seeks the will of God and surrenders to Him; one doesn't bargain with God by seeking the reward of physical healing in return for discipleship.

In the first years of my ministry an elderly retired priest opened my eyes to the divine commission to heal in the

Lord's name. I had had no seminary training. Outside of this priest and some writings of two English priests, I could find no help. Timidly I held my first services. It was the blind healing the blind. Yet God blessed those halting prayers.

How thrilled I was when I met Dr. Alfred Price and compared notes, because he, too, was feeling his way into a ministry of healing which over the years has deepened and grown in influence and helpfulness.

Now the Church has many teachers and witnesses. I thank God for such people as Agnes Sanford and her husband-priest, Father Maillard and Father Spread of England, and the whole group of people surrounding Glenn Clark.

To this list must be added Emily Gardiner Neal. Not because she is a healer or teacher, but because she bears eloquent witness: "Whereas I was blind, now I see."

WILBURN C. CAMPBELL
Bishop of West Virginia

Acknowledgments

The author is deeply grateful to the many persons without whose generous aid and co-operation this book would not have been possible.

The number of people who have contributed their time, effort, and records is too large to permit of individual mention. However, it would seem remiss not to extend special thanks to the Rev. Don H. Gross of Pittsburgh for his invaluable and time-consuming assistance throughout the preparation of the manuscript.

E. G. N.

Contents

Foreword by the Bishop of West Virginia 5

1. Spiritual Healing Today 15

2. How I First Learned of Spiritual Healing 24

3. My Investigation Gets Under Way 33

4. Additional Typical Healings 43

5. Reasons for the Decline of the Healing Ministry . . . 57

6. The Difference Between Faith Healing and Spiritual Healing 67

7. Credo 76

8. Implications of the Revival of the Healing Ministry . . 83

9. Does God Send Disease? 91

10. What Sicknesses Can Be Healed? 106

11. Your Prayer of Faith 115

12. Why Some Are Healed and Others Not 121

13. Methods of Healing Within the Church 133

14. Healing Missions 145

15. Lourdes 151

16. Christian Science and Spiritual Healing 161

17. Doctors Look At Spiritual Healing 169

18. Physics and Spiritual Healing 179

19. The Keys of the Kingdom 185

Some Books for Further Reading 191

A Reporter Finds God
Through Spiritual Healing

I

Spiritual Healing Today

THE SEEDS of this book were unknowingly sown some years ago when I inadvertently found myself at a healing service in a near-by church. Here I witnessed for the first time the phenomenon of miraculous healing.

My reaction that night was, I think, entirely typical of the uninformed skeptic. "Miracles in the twentieth century," I mocked, "the era of science and the age of reason? Complete and utter nonsense!" I saw some remarkable things happen that evening, and I took them all, not with a mere grain, but with a veritable mountain of salt!

I little guessed then that those first "miracles" were only a forerunner of the many I was to see during the months to come—the scores I was to investigate personally and have scientifically verified. Nor did I dream that what I had seen was to end in a book of this kind.

I am a professional reporter and feature writer who has worked extensively in the scientific field. All my adult life I have been a twice-a-year churchgoer. That is, I went twice a year when sufficiently pressured into it. Otherwise I went once—at Easter.

Not that I had anything against going to church—for other people, that is. As far as I was concerned, I considered it a waste of time. I rather pompously declared that I could worship better in the wide-open spaces than in a dark church listening to a dull sermon. I always neglected to add, of course, that my "wide-open spaces" consisted of the golf course, where my exclusive concern was making a hole in one!

I've been interested in science ever since I can remember. I guess you might say that science was my God. I was firmly convinced that the answers to the world's mysteries would ultimately be found in the scientific field. My experience of the past three years seems to have proved me wrong. I recognize now, and what is vastly more important, so do an increasing number of scientists, that there exists an immense spiritual world as yet untapped. In this largely undiscovered realm of the spirit lie the final answers.

I went, I saw, I examined, and eventually I believed. But make no mistake about it. Mine was no impetuous leap into faith. It was rather a painstakingly slow ascent to a then unknown summit; a climb initiated, strangely enough, by an eminent physicist who happened to remark one day at lunch that science was to a great extent based on faith.

"In order to have a starting point," he went on in explanation, "science must place its faith in certain workable hypotheses to be accepted as truth until disproved by the discovery of new evidence. Take, for example, a basic scientific axiom: the uniformity of nature. This so-called 'truth' is only hypothesis, for it is absolutely unprovable."

It was a long time after I had become convinced of the validity of spiritual healing and had unsuccessfully sought an explanation of the phenomenon in physical science, that I recalled these words. It was then that I decided to accept a workable, albeit radical, hypothesis—the hypothesis that these miracles occurring today under the revival of the Church's ancient ministry of healing are actually manifestations of the Holy Spirit, constituting demonstrable evidence of the living God.

To some, my interpretation of today's phenomena will remain an unproved theory, pure supposition. To others, I hope it will not appear in the realm of mere hypothesis, but as the immutable truth I believe it to be.

Perhaps you are not aware, as I was not, that the healing ministry of the Church is as old as the Church itself. Our ignorance is excusable, for that ancient ministry had declined over the centuries into virtual nonexistence. During the past few years it has been revived, with, to me, incredibly exciting results.

Although the renascence of the healing ministry has not come about through the sole efforts of any one denomination, it is understandable that the Episcopal Church should have taken the lead in reactivating its dormant ministry of healing. While for centuries largely in disuse, this healing ministry was never wholly lost, remaining throughout the ages as part of the official ministry of the Episcopal Church. As a consequence, this denomination has today the most widespread and active healing ministry in the United States. But it does not stand alone. Dr. Leslie B. Weatherhead, renowned Methodist Churchman, has said, "The Church *must* be called back to its healing ministry." At last, throughout Christendom it is being gradually realized that Christ's commission to His Church was twofold: to preach and *to heal*. "And he sent them to preach the kingdom of God, and to heal the sick" (Luke 9:2).

As more and more churches all over the world seek to carry out the divine commission in its entirety, it becomes clear that the gift of healing was never withdrawn from the Church. It was simply misplaced over the ages. It belongs again to any church which wishes to claim it.

The Methodist Church is not far behind the Episcopal in its healing work. Dr. W. E. Sangster, M.A., able Methodist spokesman, states that keen and informed minds today are convinced that Christ commissioned His Church to heal the sick. An impressive number of his colleagues who share this conviction are acting upon it.

The recollection that John Wesley himself was a teacher of and firm believer in divine healing has given impetus to the Methodists' increasingly active healing ministry. Today's Methodist is reading with new interest the words of Wesley's journal: "Pain in the head and back, with fever," he wrote in 1791. "Had to lie down . . . pain, pain and coughing. These words came to mind strongly: 'These things shall follow them that believe.' Prayed and called on Jesus to increase my faith and to confirm the word of grace. Whilst I was speaking, my pain vanished and the fever left me."

The Lutherans, too, have a precedent for today's healing in Martin Luther's often repeated saying that if we have faith enough to be healed, there is no disease from which we may not recover. They read new meaning in his words: "Heavy thoughts bring on physical maladies. When the soul is oppressed, so is the body."

The Rev. Roland Brown of Chicago, a great Baptist leader in the healing ministry, has made his entire church body conscious of its Christ-inspired function: to teach, to preach, and *to heal.*

The eminent Presbyterian, the Rev. Frank Riale, author of the book *Divine Antidote to Sin, Sickness and Death,* has laid the groundwork for Presbyterian healing work by pointing out that God is *not* the author of sin and disease and by His power can overcome both. Miraculous healing in the Roman Catholic Church is by no means confined to its great shrines such as Lourdes and St. Anne de Beaupré. Priests like Father James Cox of St. Patrick's in Pittsburgh have conducted dramatic healing ministries within their local parish churches.

The Quakers are doing an outstanding work in the field of spiritual healing, as are the Pentecostal Church, the Evangelical and Reformed Church, and many small cults and sects which emphasize the healing ministry with magnificent results.

Dr. Norman Vincent Peale, renowned spiritual leader and pastor of the Marble Collegiate Church in New York, has made a noteworthy contribution in the field of healing by the institution of healing services in his church. He speaks for many clergymen all over the nation when he says: "I think there will be great progress in the coming years in spiritual healing—for we are just beginning to understand the fundamental laws of the spirit."

Participation of so many churches in the revival of the healing ministry makes the healing movement almost world-wide in scope so far as representation goes, but it is still far from universal. Only when every church in Christendom accepts its divine commission to heal and returns again to one of the most vital branches of the ministry, can the full effect of the power and love of Christ be universally realized—an effect which staggers the imagination. Already, as more and more churches join in this great healing revival and strive in increasing numbers to fulfill His commission to preach the Word and heal the sick, countless people are being regenerated spiritually as well as physically by their new vision. They are seeing the New Testament in its intended light.

The Good News is no longer a myth, an intangible and hopeless promise. It is a promise now fulfilled, and by its fulfillment, the hidden hunger of mankind for demonstrable evidence of the love of God is gradually being allayed.

Psychosomatic medicine is, of course, neither new nor revolutionary. Plato in the fourth century B.C. wrote, "He that will cure the body must cure the Soul—that is, must bring the mind to a temperature, a moderation, an equanimity." Today psychosomatic medicine for the treatment of psychosomatic disease is an established scientific practice.

But what of organic and congenital ailments? Will balanced emotions cure a cancer or heal a tubercular lesion? Will mental equilibrium straighten a club foot or snap into place a congenitally dislocated hip?

Every ailment and disease known to man is responding today to a great outside power manifested under the revived ministry of spiritual healing. No one can wholly explain the phenomena of healing which are occurring, but no one who takes the time and trouble to investigate can deny their occurrence.

My research has been objective. I approached the subject with an open mind—or as open a mind as an unbeliever in the twentieth century could reasonably be expected to have. My skepticism made me extremely cautious in accepting any healing claims without ample and what appeared incontrovertible medical verification. Today I make no pretense of having an "open" mind. I *know* beyond the shadow of any doubt that these miracles are happening.

Obviously this does not mean that everyone who claims a healing has been miraculously healed. I have reviewed many cases where there was no reason to believe that a cure had been effected. In some instances, these claimed healings were the result of wishful thinking; in some, the result of hysteria; in a few, the desire of the individuals to stand for a short time in the limelight.

Such false claims are an inevitable part of the healing picture, which is why considerable caution must be exercised in any appraisal of the subject. If my initial skepticism made me cautious in the beginning, my faith makes me doubly so now, for there is always the grave danger that the working of the Holy Spirit can be misused and prostituted into chicanery.

The attitude of a growing number of scientists toward spiritual healing is interesting and significant. Most men who have investigated the subject are in accord with the physicist, noted for his work on the atom bomb, who comments: "The word 'miracle' may not be in the lexicon of the scientist, but these phenomena of healing are occurring in sufficient number to warrant the serious attention of scientists everywhere. In view of the nature of so many of these healings, I am convinced that the presently accepted laws of physics must ultimately be completely revolutionized."

Perhaps the most cogent testimony to the widespread effectiveness of the revived ministry of spiritual healing is the interest it has awakened in the medical field. Within the past few months there have been held three seminars in Rye, New York, where for the first time in history a substantial number of doctors and psychologists have met with clergymen of every denomination to discuss the acknowledged phenomenon of spiritual healing. As religion itself has become increasingly intellectually "respectable," so is spiritual healing being recognized as a credible and impressive branch of the Church's ministry.

Doctors who a short while ago would have scoffed at the mention of spiritual healing are now working in close cooperation with many of the Church's healing commissions and clinics. A number of physicians, intrigued by the healings they have witnessed, are now working on Dr. J. B. Rhine's parapsychology staff, seeking to learn more of the phenomenon.

As one physician states: "Extreme caution is necessary in evaluating spiritual healing. However, as men of science, we doctors must face the truth: non-medical healings are actually taking place. An impressive number appear to be genuine healings of organic and congenital ailments; cures which appear to be neither the fancied result of wishful thinking, nor religious hysteria. Those of us in medicine who have impartially investigated the subject are now pretty well convinced that man is a trinity, composed of body, mind, and spirit. Important as are the medically induced cures of mind and body, they cannot be wholly effective without a healing of the spirit." With this dictum the British Medical Journal seems in agreement when it states: "There is no tissue of the human body wholly removed from the influence of spirit."

Many have been brought to God by the touch of His healing hand. Thousands more have been brought to Him by their witness of His love. I am one of those thousands.

I have never been miraculously healed, but I have known

a greater miracle. By His grace I have discovered that faith can be a higher faculty than reason; that there is a greater knowledge than that of the mind—the knowledge of the heart; and that there is a higher truth than that of science—the truth of the spirit. This book is the story of my discovery.

2

How I First Learned
of Spiritual Healing

IT ALL began with a telephone call on a cold February
night. "The car battery's dead, they can't send a taxi
for an hour, and I'm due at an important meeting at
8 P.M.," came my new neighbor's harried voice over the
wire. "Could you possibly run me over? It won't take over
twenty minutes, and I'll get a taxi back."

I rather reluctantly acquiesced. After all, I scarcely
knew the man. I was busy trying to meet a deadline, and
the roads were a glare of ice.

I didn't know much about my new neighbor except that
he was vice-president of a corporation in town. He seemed
nice enough, although I had already catalogued him as
being a bit on the peculiar side. I remembered, as I walked
out to the garage, how he had been all excited one day
about a "healing" his wife was supposed to have received
somewhere. I hadn't paid too much attention at the time,
instantly putting him down as some sort of crackpot.

He joined me as I got to the car. "Say, it's nice of you
to do this for me," he said. "My little girl's sick in the
hospital with meningitis. Our minister was there this afternoon and laid on hands. She improved right afterwards,
but the doctor said it was just temporary. He said there

wasn't much hope. My wife's at the hospital now. I just felt certain that if I went to the healing service tonight and prayed for her, she'd be all right. As a sign of active faith, I wanted to get to the church myself."

I stopped short in my mental tracks. What sort of gibberish was this? Who *were* these queer people who were now my next door neighbors?

"What church do you want to go to?" I asked as I started the engine, half hoping it wouldn't turn over. When he mentioned the local Episcopal church I was surprised. I'd always thought of Episcopalians as ultra-dignified, super-conservative people—stuffed shirt, if you will. What were they doing holding "healing" services? They must have loaned the church. That was the answer.

Beyond a few perfunctory questions about his daughter's condition (under the circumstances I was relieved to find that she was in the care of my own physician whom I considered tops), my companion and I rode in silence.

By the time we drew up to the church, it had started to snow. I knew in this weather it would be impossible to get a cab after the service, so after ascertaining that the affair wouldn't last over an hour, I volunteered to wait and drop the man off at the hospital on the way home. The problem now was what to do with myself while he was in church. Driving conditions were so bad it wasn't worthwhile to go home and come back. I finally accepted, with rather poor grace, I'm afraid, my companion's suggestion that I accompany him to the service. The church would at least provide warm shelter for an hour.

We parked the car a block away and walked back to the church, fighting the wind every step of the way. A lot of people, as undiscouraged by the vicious weather as my friend, were trooping up the church steps.

We slipped into the first pew we came to with two empty seats. I glanced at the woman on my left as I sat down, noticing that she seemed to have a large goiter. Something about her looked vaguely familiar.

The service opened with a hymn and a brief prayer. Then there was a short talk on spiritual healing, by the priest.

He pointed out that if you believed that Christ's commission to His Church was to preach the Kingdom of God, you must also believe that His commission was to heal, for the two commands were inseparable: "Then he called his twelve disciples together, and gave them power and authority over all devils, and to cure diseases. And he sent them to *preach the Kingdom of God,* and to *heal the sick*" (Luke 9:1, 2).

The clergyman's remarks were founded on the basic premise that the healing power of Christ through the Father was as evident today as it was nearly two thousand years ago. I remember that he emphasized the fact that Jesus is the same, yesterday, today, and forever—and so are His works. There is no "day" of miracles, any more than there is a limited "time" of Christ.

He spoke of the power of the redemptive love of Christ, which is the healing power, and which is available to all who seek it through faith and repentance. "And the prayer of faith shall save the sick, and the Lord shall raise him up; and if he have committed sins, they shall be forgiven him" (James 5:15).

Obviously this was no place for me. I couldn't even accept the facts upon which the priest's basic premise had been predicated. I believed in some nebulous sort of "Creator"; I believed that Jesus was a great ethical and moral leader. I was far from sure that He was the Son of God, and I had never pretended to believe in the so-called miracles of His earthly ministry. Whenever I had bothered to think about it, which wasn't often, I explained the "miracles" away as psychological aberrations. If I couldn't believe in miracles occurring two thousand years ago, I certainly wasn't going to believe in any purported miracles occurring today!

I gave the clergyman credit for sincerity, thought the congregation over-zealous, to put it mildly, and closed my eyes.

Next thing I knew, I heard the clergyman summon those who sought healing, either for their souls or bodies, themselves or others, to the Altar rail, for the laying-on-of-hands and Holy Communion.

I watched as one by one the congregation filed quietly to the Altar, noticing particularly one small, red-headed boy who passed close by me, his hands a mass of warts.

I watched the believers kneeling at the Altar, and almost against my will I began to stop feeling supercilious.

The atmosphere was strangely charged with what seemed an almost palpable faith. An air of expectancy began to flood the dimly lit church. Suddenly it was no longer expectancy. It was absolute certitude.

I listened to the priest as he laid his hands upon the head of each supplicant, intoning: "I lay my hand upon thee in the Name of the Father, and of the Son, and of the Holy Ghost; beseeching the mercy of our Lord Jesus Christ, that all thy pain and sickness of body being put to flight, the blessing of health may be restored unto thee. In the Name of Jesus, be thou healed."

In this company of the faithful, I felt myself an undesirable alien. I may have been no churchgoer, but neither was I a blasphemer. I felt my presence at this service to be a sort of sacrilege. For the first time in many years, I found myself praying—to whom, I wasn't sure. "If there is a God, don't let these people down," I pleaded. "*Please* don't let them down, but honor their faith." It was not until some months later that I realized the absurd incongruity of an unbeliever praying to a God he didn't think existed for the benefit of this large group of men and women who knew more of faith than I could ever learn.

I heard the words: "Go, believing that thou art healed." One by one those at the Altar returned to their pews. They walked back, heads high, in quiet dignity and full confidence.

As the small boy with the warts brushed by me, I looked at his hands, but he passed too quickly for me to see them. I flinched as he touched me from the burning heat of his body. The thought flashed through my mind that he shouldn't be here with a temperature of at least 103.

The woman sitting beside me dropped to her knees in prayer. Although we were not touching, it seemed as if I could feel an excessive and tremendous heat emanating from her body. I thought briefly that the health authorities should step in and stop these fevered individuals from exposing others to their obviously acute infections. I glanced surreptitiously at her throat—and my heart began to pound. I could see no evidence of the swelling which I had been so sure was there a short while before.

My friend rejoined me, his eyes wet, but shining with a look of such bare joy that I looked down in embarrassment—and no little apprehension. What would he do if his little girl had died while we were in church?

The congregation knelt again for the blessing, and the service was over.

In walking out of the church, I looked curiously and closely at the woman who had been sitting next to me. There was no doubt of it; her neck was completely normal. "My imagination is certainly getting the better of me," I thought. "There was probably nothing wrong with her in the first place."

The small boy was ahead of me, now holding his father's arm. I looked at his exposed hand. I blinked and looked again. It was brown, and smooth as silk. No sign of a wart anywhere. I had the distinctly uncanny feeling that either all this was a dream, or I was losing my mind.

My neighbor and I walked down the church steps, struggling to keep our footing against the wind. Once in the car, I attempted to be casual. "Does this sort of thing go on often?" I asked.

"The healing services are held here once a week," came the reply, "and that's why I was so anxious to come tonight. Next week might have been too late."

Noting my look of bewilderment, my friend continued: "Of course the healing power of Christ is available to everyone, everywhere, but the power is strengthened by corporate faith. I needed the faith of others to strengthen my own faith tonight and now I wonder why. The second I knelt at the Altar I knew that my little girl would be all right."

I left my friend off at the hospital as arranged, and went

on home. I tried to finish my work, but I was too excited and puzzled by what I had seen—or did I just *think* I had seen it?

Had I imagined the little boy's warts? No—I was sure not—but I had read somewhere of psychosomatic cures for this condition. Besides, warts came and went spontaneously. The fact that these chose to disappear in the middle of a "healing" service was purely coincidental.

The swelling I thought I had observed in the neck of the woman next to me might well have been imagined. The light was dim, and she wore a fur collar which might well have cast a shadow on her throat. And as for my neighbor's child, I only hoped she *would* be all right. Of course, if she were, that too was undoubtedly coincidence. Patients frequently take a sudden and unanticipated turn for the better. Yes, just as I had always contended, there's a rational explanation for everything under the sun.

About midnight I decided to call my neighbor. After all, I told myself, it was only courteous to evince a friendly interest in his little girl. I didn't add, even to myself, that I was insatiably curious to find out just what had happened.

He answered the phone at once, and I knew by his voice that all was well.

"Say, I want to thank you again for taking me . . ." he began. I cut him short. "What about the child?" I asked.

"She's just fine," he replied. "They can't understand at the hospital what happened—that is, nobody but our doctor can. Funny thing, but he doesn't seem surprised."

No wonder, I thought. He probably knew she had a fifty-fifty chance. She just passed some sort of crisis in ner illness, that's all. Why was *my* heart beating faster than usual?

In the cold, clear light of the next morning, I marvelled at my excitement of the night before. The whole thing now seemed obvious: any ailments "cured" at these services were imaginary; any "healings" received, purely psychological. I granted that there was a strong possibility of psychotherapeutic benefit resulting from such "healing" services—that is, if people did not go overboard and refuse medical care—and I would concede that certain types of psychosomatic ailments might respond favorably to this type of psychosomatic treatment; but that any true organic or congenital disease could be healed through a church service was manifestly absurd.

It was perhaps ten days later that I lunched with my doctor, a close personal friend. Towards the end of the meal, he made some reference to my new neighbors, who were also his patients. "Remarkable recovery that child made," he said. "We'd done all we could do for her medically. She just didn't respond. Scientifically speaking, she didn't have a chance—but now she's fully recovered. You could almost say it was a miracle."

I good-naturedly chided him, a medical man, for his choice of the word "miracle."

"That's about the only word you *can* use in a case like this," he commented dryly. "And this is not by any means the first I've seen."

I told him, then, of my involuntary attendance at the healing service ten days before. When I was through, he nodded. "I can't explain it," he said, "but these things *are* happening." He went on to relate several medically inexplicable healings which had occurred among his patients, including one apparently instantaneous healing of a carefully diagnosed inoperable cancer.

"As an example of what's going on," he said, "I saw a woman day before yesterday who was scheduled to go in for a goiter operation today. She went to a service last week, and claimed her goiter spontaneously disappeared. All I know is, there wasn't a sign of it when I examined her two days ago."

I looked up startled. "Was she a small woman, dark eyes and hair? Did she wear a gray coat with a large fur collar?" The doctor nodded. "Yes. Mrs. J. She lives down the street from you. Do you know her?"

"I sat beside her when she was healed," I said.

The excitement I felt is hard to describe. I was still skeptical. The best doctors can be mistaken, and one swallow, or even two or three, doesn't make a Spring. However, if a medical man of good reputation dared acknowledge these healing phenomena, there *could* be something to it.

One thing was sure: it would make a whale of a story if there were any facts at all to back it up. I decided then and there to do some investigating.

3

My Investigation Gets Under Way

M Y FIRST step was to attend a number of healing services in various churches, in order to make sure that the apparent healings were occurring on a sufficiently wide scale to justify even a cursory investigation. At the end of two months, I was satisfied that what I had seen that first night with my neighbor was not due to the hypnotic influence of a fanatical clergyman on a peculiarly susceptible group of individuals. Alleged healings were occurring in many different churches, and I was anxious to explore what appeared to be an extensive phenomenon.

In contacting those local clergymen who practiced the healing ministry, I freely acknowledged that I was not a believer. Without equivocation I stated my purpose: as a reporter I was out to prove or disprove the validity of some of the many healings being claimed.

I found both the clergymen and laymen involved undismayed by my skepticism and unafraid of my proposed investigation. Not only were they willing to co-operate, but in most cases they exerted considerable time and effort in helping me to procure the type of unimpeachable evidence I required.

That this evidence was going to be difficult to obtain was obvious from the start. Hospital medical records are not the property of the patient and are therefore not available to him or to anyone else without complete co-operation of both the hospital and the doctor in charge. This joint co-operation was always difficult and frequently impossible to procure. However, laboratory reports indicating the patient's former condition and attesting to his subsequent improvement or cure following his alleged spiritual healing were produced in sufficient number to provide impressive substantiation of the claimed non-medical cures.

When these medical reports were made unavailable, the doctor in charge of a particular patient was contacted and asked to confirm his original diagnosis and any subsequent change in the patient's condition after the supposed spiritual healing. A number of doctors complied with this request in the same manner as the physician of a woman patient for whom an operation had been scheduled. Her bladder had dropped, causing it to protrude through her vagina. On March 4, 1952, the doctor issued a written report of her condition. Eight days later, after her claimed healing, he re-examined her and reported in writing: "The patient was found to be much improved." In the interests of accuracy, it should be stated that the woman had been entirely healed, and the previously scheduled operation was cancelled as being unnecessary.

Many doctors refused to issue even so cautious a statement as the one just quoted. They claimed that such an admission of sudden improvement over the former condition would, in many cases, imply "miraculous" healing, and any such implication "could get me into serious trouble with the American Medical Association." At my insistence, some of these physicians were willing to give me a written statement as to the *present* condition of the patient, but only a verbal acknowledgment of the original diagnosis. A typical case involved a male patient who had suffered for some years from extreme hypertension, and as a result had a greatly enlarged heart. He was examined in January, 1953. Two weeks later he claimed a spiritual healing. The doctor re-examined him and issued the following statement: "I have examined Mr. Y. and found him in good physical condition. Blood pressure 130 over 70; heart near normal."

A number of physicians preferred still another approach. They were willing to confirm their *original* diagnosis, but refused to state that any type of healing had occurred. However, in those cases where the patient's cure was perceptible to even the most casual observer, I accepted as trustworthy evidence the original diagnosis and the patient's present obvious lack of symptoms. A characteristic case was that of a woman who, according to her doctor, had been badly crippled with arthritis. Her joints had been extremely swollen, and she could walk only with the aid of two canes. When I noted that after her alleged healing she was able to walk, erect and free, with no evidence of swelling in any joints, I was willing to concede the validity of her healing.

In cases involving surgery, the patient's story as to operative procedure and medical findings was verified wherever possible by the participating doctors. In some such cases the testimonies of clergymen, friends, family, and outside agencies constituted an authoritative contribution to the healing picture. One of the first cases I investigated provides a good example of what I mean and also illustrates why an honest appraisal of spiritual healing must consider not only the evidence offered by a few isolated cases, but the massive cumulative evidence which can only be derived from the study of hundreds of claimed healings.

A woman who had been ill since the recent death of her sister from cancer was suddenly seized with severe abdominal pain. Her family physician diagnosed the trouble as appendicitis, and an operation was immediately scheduled. Twenty minutes after the patient had entered the operating room, the surgeon sent for her family. He came straight to the point. "Send for her husband from overseas at once. She has cancer, and we must operate again next week." The husband was reached through the Red Cross and immediately started for home.

The woman's former rector was advised of the gravity of her condition, and held a prayer service in his church the day before the operation. That same day, her family attended the healing service in their local parish church. Immediately following the service, the clergyman proceeded to the hospital where he administered Holy Communion and the laying-on-of-hands. "The minute he touched my head," said the woman, "I felt relaxed and unworried for the first time since entering the hospital. To the nurses' amazement I fell asleep and slept the whole night through."

The patient entered surgery at 8 A.M. At 8:45 A.M. she was wheeled back from the operating room. Her apprehensive family intercepted the two surgeons as they walked down the corridor. "She's fine," one of them said, his face beaming. "No cancer at all." The other spoke up: "I'm frank to admit that this is the happiest mistake in my career!"

It seems that when the incision had been reopened for the second operation, the surgeons had discovered that the "malignant" tumor had shrunk to one-third its former size, and was now palpably soft, instead of hard as before. The tissue was again biopsied, and this time the report came back negative. Today, five years later, the woman is in good health.

Her doctors claimed a mistaken diagnosis, and at that time this certainly seemed to me a plausible enough explanation. However, the very next case I investigated caused me to wonder. It, too, concerned an alleged cancer healing, this time cancer of the lung. The diagnosis had been based on an extensive series of X-ray, bronchoscopy, and sputum tests—all positive. As a result, the patient was scheduled for resection of five ribs and removal of the affected lung.

Shortly before the operation was to be performed, the patient attended a healing service and claimed a cure. When he returned to the hospital for final examination prior to surgery, a repetition of the previously conducted tests revealed no evidence of lung cancer. He was dismissed from the hospital, and is today in robust health.

The medical explanation was, again, mistaken diagnosis. Taking into account the number and variety of diagnostic tests which had been performed, the sudden remission of all previous symptoms, the dramatic physical change of a man desperately ill to one in glowing health, this explanation appeared to me suspiciously inadequate.

Now I have a profound admiration for the medical profession, but by the time I had examined some twenty similar cases, I began to grow irritated with the glib and monotonous refrain, "wrong diagnosis." I finally pointed out to one of these doctors that he and his co-workers were indicting the medical profession for criminal incompetency, for within my small orbit, within a few weeks, had fallen nearly two dozen cases where the mistake in diagnosis would, at best, have permanently invalided the patient by drastic and unnecessary surgery; and at worst, would have cost him his life.

In those cases where doctors and hospitals have refused co-operation, the original disability has been clearly stated in Workmen's Compensation reports and similar documents. The intensity of the medical examination which always precedes the issuing of a disability pension seemed to me reliable proof of the genuineness of the former ailment. Time after time I have seen cases like that of the man who sustained an accidental injury in his work, suffering the total loss of use of one of his limbs. After careful examination by six doctors who testified to his permanent disability, he was awarded full compensation.

This man, and so many like him, was able to resume strenuous physical labor after his healing three years ago, with full use of the disabled limb restored. This constituted, in my eyes, incontrovertible evidence of his recovery.

As time went on, the variety of evidence attesting to former illness and medically unlikely cure left little doubt in my mind that some extraordinary healing force was in operation. Also, as time went on, I was to observe a noteworthy change of attitude among many doctors. An increasing number now refrained from claiming a wrong diagnosis, and said instead, "It looks like a miracle—but don't quote me!"

Not only did more physicians seem willing to testify to the validity of certain non-medical healings, but over the past year, members of the medical profession have called to my attention healings which they frankly acknowledged seemed to be of "miraculous" nature. Typical of these is a case reported by a New York doctor which concerns his own wife.

"She had been in labor with our first child for sixty-one hours, and she was as near dead as I have ever seen anyone, before or since, who didn't die. It is my sincere belief that it was the prayers of five of our friends, who had met together when they learned of her desperate condition, which turned the tide.

"As a final effort to save the mother's life, the attending physician prepared to decapitate the infant. Just as he was about to proceed, the baby emerged. Immediately afterwards, the mother went into profound shock and was practically dead. I am completely convinced that it was the power of God, rather than the power of medical science as we understand it today, which made her recovery possible."

Was this just chance? Would the woman have lived anyway? Perhaps, but what about all the other cases of medically inexplicable recoveries submitted to me by other doctors?

Take, for example, the boy involved in an automobile accident. He was thrown out of the car, which landed on top of him. His back was crushed, and he was bleeding profusely and extensively. Taken to a near-by hospital, he lay unconscious for many weeks, paralyzed from the neck down. According to the doctors, his case was completely hopeless. The only person *not* hopeless was his minister, who went each day to the hospital to pray for him.

At last the boy regained consciousness, and the clergyman confidently expressed his conviction that God would heal him. The doctors were extremely critical, objecting that it was barbaric cruelty to assure an obviously hopeless case of recovery.

One day, about two weeks after the patient had emerged from coma, he received the laying-on-of-hands and felt a sensation like "liquid fire running through my body." Three weeks later he got out of bed and walked. He re-entered college the next fall and graduated a year later with highest honors.

Was this, too, just chance? What then of the case reported by yet another doctor?

"B. D., age 3. March 2, 1952. This little girl leaned over the stove and her dress caught fire. She was brought into my office severely burned. Sent at once to County Hospital. Parents were told that the burn was extremely serious, involving 40% of the child's body area. A burn of that extent in a child of this size is considered a fatal burn.

"The next night the child started to have a series of convulsions, and the parents were told that she might die in any one of these. All nourishment was by vein. I knew that medical science was now helpless in this case. That night my wife and I decided to try God. My wife, who is a registered nurse, was trying to visualize a healthy kidney function in this little child, when suddenly, instead of the little blackened child, she saw a normal, healthy, beautiful one. In my own case, I tried to pour God's love and power into the child. Suddenly there was a tremendous feeling of life and power that made me tingle all over, and I suddenly knew with complete conviction that there was a change in the child's condition. This was about 10:30 P.M. The next morning the child was distinctly better, and taking fluids by mouth. The house surgeon remarked to the mother, 'I don't for the life of me know why the child is here. Those burns were fatal!'

"The child made an uneventful recovery, and has had several skin graft operations since, and is now a well child."

Scores of such verifiable healings, reported by reputable doctors, induced me to believe that these healings were not mere happenstance.

At the end of a few months I noted that this strange healing force worked in curiously different ways. Some healings occurred through absent prayer, the patient miles away. Some were instant and complete; others were delayed and gradual. In most cases of spiritual healing, the defective organ supposedly causing the illness was restored to normal function, but in a few instances the individual attained complete health in *spite* of the fact that the original condition of the organ remained ostensibly unchanged after the healing.

Several cases were brought to my attention of that amazing manifestation of the healing force which results in the physical evidence of surgery, when none has taken place. In one instance, for example, a woman was spiritually healed of a breast tumor. Immediately after her healing, a scar became visible. A case of somewhat similar nature is reliably reported by Elsie Salmon in her book, *He Heals Today*. A sinus condition was spiritually healed. The power on the antrum bone was so great that it left burn marks on the patient's cheeks.

In an effort to shed some light on the healing phenomenon, I searched continuously for some evidence of a general, underlying psychic factor—some common quality of personality, perhaps, which might make those healed peculiarly susceptible to the healing power, whatever it was and wherever it came from. I could find no such common denominator. Those healed were "all sorts and conditions of men." They came from every walk of life. They were of varying degrees of intelligence and different levels of education. They were of many diverse temperaments. Only after, and as a result of, healing was there a discernible common bond: a joyous faith in God, founded on the conviction shared by day laborer and professional man alike, that His mysteries cannot be intellectualized.

4

Additional Typical Healings

AS A MATTER of interest, I cite here a few typical healings selected at random from among the hundreds in my files.

Case #56 . . . J. H., age 15 months. Diagnosis: acute lymphatic leukemia. He was admitted to hospital acutely ill and in convulsions. He became increasingly anemic, his hemoglobin dropping to 35% of normal. Repeated transfusions had no effect on blood count, and his course was steadily downhill. He was then put at the center of a church group's healing prayers, while several individuals held him in their worship. He immediately began to improve, and was subsequently discharged from the hospital with a normal blood count. From the delicate, sickly child he had always been, he emerged a normal, robust little boy.

Case #42 . . . Mrs. L. B., age 33, and her son, Jimmy, age 8. In 1947, Jimmy had suffered an attack of rheumatic fever. Since that time he had been invalided; X-rays and cardiograms revealed a hugely enlarged heart, two bad valves, and a stricture. In 1952, the mother contracted rheumatic fever. Critically ill for some weeks, she was ordered to remain in bed for twelve months. Financially unable to procure help to care for her invalid son, arrangements were made to admit Jimmy to the Children's Convalescent Hospital for Crippled Children until his mother was herself well and able to resume his care.

At this time a friend introduced the mother to spiritual healing, a subject about which she knew nothing. The night before Jimmy entered the hospital, healing prayers were offered for both mother and son.

The following afternoon the hospital's heart specialist called Mrs. L. B. to state that the X-rays and cardiogram just completed revealed that Jimmy's heart was perfectly normal. He claimed that a wrong diagnosis must have been made. At the mother's insistence, he called the noted heart specialist who had originally diagnosed Jimmy's condition, and had that diagnosis confirmed. He also called the boy's pediatrician, who confirmed the fact that he had examined Jimmy the day before he entered the hospital and had found his previous condition unchanged. The hospital physician could only say, "It looks like a miracle." Jimmy was swimming and riding a bicycle before the summer was over, and attended school, for the first time in his life, the next fall. He has been well and strong for the past three years.

Mrs. L. B. was also healed. Within two weeks she was up and around and within a month was carrying on with unrestricted activity.

Case #47 . . . S. R., age 9 months. Diagnosis: nephritis, following pneumonia. Laboratory tests revealed destruction of kidney tissue. The child's legs were badly swollen and were filled with fluid. Discomfort was relieved by tapping, but doctor advised that condition was final stage of dropsy.

No cure possible because of extensive kidney tissue destruction.

Healing prayers were offered on a Friday. When the child was taken to the doctor on the following Monday, the legs were completely normal. The doctor remarked that "only a miracle could have caused this change in condition." Five years after the healing, the child is still completely well, kidneys functioning normally.

Case #59 ... age 9 hours. Diagnosis: congenital intestinal obstruction. The physician advised parents shortly after baby's birth that her condition was critical and surgery must be done in an attempt to save her life. Just before the operation began, the parents called on various groups for healing prayers to be added to their own.

The surgeons found the nature of the operation even more severe than they had anticipated. Three times during the two hours and thirty minutes ordeal, they reported that the infant had died on the table. Three times revived, the child left the operating room alive to make a "surprisingly uneventful recovery." Two years later she is still in robust health.

Case #71 . . . L. E., age 57. Diagnosis: far advanced rheumatoid arthritis. This woman underwent surgery five years ago. Dissatisfied with her recovery, the operating surgeon talked with his patient at some length and discovered that she was filled with a deep inner hostility. It was he who brought to her attention the fact of spiritual healing. He explained its fundamentals, and healing prayers were said for her recovery. Within three days the arthritis was completely gone, and also the Heberden's nodes (those hard nodules about the hands, etc., which one frequently sees in such cases of advanced rheumatoid arthritis).

Case #68 . . . G. W., age 15. Diagnosis: Hodgkin's disease. Three months after recovery from scarlet fever, the glands in patient's neck began to swell. Condition grew steadily worse, until the boy was unable to walk because of shortness of breath. He was then confined to bed, but unable to lie down, day or night, because of difficulty in breathing. He was entered in a large city hospital, where a noted doctor took charge of his case. X-rays were taken, and the glands from each side of his neck were removed. His parents were advised that he had Hodgkin's disease, incurable, and that he had not long to live. He was taken home to die.

The boy's father was an atheist, but his mother was a deeply religious woman. She and the local minister asked the congregation to pray for a healing.

The boy seemed to grow progressively weaker after his return from the hospital. After he had been home about two weeks, his mother sat beside his bed and said, "I know now that you are going to get well. Your father disappeared this afternoon, and we found him in a corner of the farm, praying for the first time in his life."

Next day an eminent doctor drove up to the farm, having been sent by a friend of the family. After thorough examination, he ordered the boy back to the hospital for immediate surgery. He said to the mother, "I will operate, but the boy is so far gone, I must tell you that his life is in the hands of the Lord—not mine. Tell everyone you know to pray for him."

The operation was performed, and the doctor sat at the patient's bedside for fourteen hours, in constant prayer with the boy's parents. When he left, he said, "Your son will live—but you must understand that the spark of life left was not preserved by me. It is your prayers which have given him the chance to live."

The boy startled the hospital staff by making a speedy and uneventful recovery. Today, some years later, he is in perfect health.

Case #54 . . . J. P., age 46. Diagnosis: ulcer of the eye. The patient was scheduled for surgery to remove ulcer. A week before the operation, he received the laying-on-of-hands. Later on that same day he was visited by his doctor who was amazed to find the eye suddenly and dramatically improved. The laying-on-of-hands was repeated twice within the next week. The eye condition was completely healed, and the operation cancelled.

Case #58 . . . M. R., age 41. Diagnosis: cancer. This woman, suffering from advanced cancer, had been operated upon in a final effort to save her life. She had delayed too long. The operation proved hopeless, and the doctors informed her family that she could not be expected to live for more than a few days. Her clergyman was called. He proceeded at once to the hospital, where he administered Holy Communion and anointed the patient. Within half an hour the patient began to rally. She improved steadily, and within two weeks walked out of the hospital. Two years later she is in good health, with no indication of the malignancy which had "spread throughout her body."

Case #38 . . . Mrs. T. S., age 42. Diagnosis: malignant breast tumor. Patient was in hospital awaiting surgery— mastectomy (removal of breast). Healing prayers were being offered. She was prepared for operation, wheeled down to operating theatre, and given a general anaesthetic. The surgeon could find no trace of a lump of any kind in her breast.

Case #27 . . . B. W., age 48. Diagnosis: stomach ulcer of fifteen years' duration. The patient, at the instigation of friends, attended a healing service. He was in considerable distress when entering the church and was skeptical of healing. While kneeling at the Altar, he suddenly became conscious of an inflowing of spiritual power, and at the same time, the total surcease of all pain. His healing was instant and complete. He has had no recurrence of the trouble for over four years.

Case #62 . . . R. N., age 50. Diagnosis: heart block and tremendous enlargement of the heart. The doctors imposed the usual restrictions indicated in a case of this sort, ordering a completely revised life which would preclude all excitement, haste, and heavy labor. Just at this time, the patient felt himself called to a type of work which meant everything the doctors had advised against. He prayed over his decision and finally said, "All right, Lord. I think you mean me to go. I am yours from here on out."

The man was spiritually healed a short while later. He has been examined by the best doctors in his city, by every instrument and test. His heart is entirely normal in every respect.

Case #86 . . . W. H. Diagnosis: coronary thrombosis. The patient was stricken while sitting in a hammock in his back yard. His attending physician is one of the outstanding diagnosticians of the southwest. After many weeks in bed and four months of absolute rest, the patient was permitted to resume his work on a greatly restricted basis. About eight months after his attack, he learned of spiritual healing. He was subsequently instantly and completely cured through the healing ministry of the Church. Not only was his healing verifiable by cardiogram, but his extraordinarily active life during the past five years attests to his exceptionally robust health.

Case #74 . . . F. F., age 68. Diagnosis: fungus growth on left eye. Prognosis by two leading ophthalmologists: eventual blindness. Patient received laying-on-of-hands, and growth instantly disappeared. No recurrence after three years.

Case #65 . . . Diagnosis: tuberculosis. The patient was sent by his doctors to the mountains near San Diego. While there he learned of spiritual healing. Several weeks later he asked that the rector of a San Diego church anoint him for healing. His wife knelt with him as he was anointed. Immediately after receiving the Sacrament, he returned home and telephoned his doctor long distance that he was returning to his old home to resume his work. The doctor was shocked, saying that he was taking his life in his hands.

Within two weeks all symptoms of hoarseness and coughing had ceased, his temperature was normal, and he was working a full day with no fatigue. At his sister's request, he was carefully examined at the local hospital. The report came back that the lungs showed old scars, but were completely healed. There was no recurrence of tuberculosis.

Case #61 . . . G. P., age 37. Diagnosis: tuberculosis. X-rays and sputum tests made two days before alleged spiritual healing revealed active tuberculosis of right lung. Same tests two days after healing revealed "old" scars, lung completely healed.

Case #36 . . . W. J., age 16. Diagnosis: blood clot on the brain. The patient hit his head on a rock while diving. He was rushed to hospital where diagnosis was made, and his family and clergyman were summoned immediately. Doctors gave him about an hour to live. When the clergyman arrived, the parents were pacing up and down the hospital corridor, while two doctors and several nurses worked over the boy. The minister entered the room, held the boy's hand, and said, "The Lord is right here watching over you. Just close your eyes and ask His help." The patient relaxed, the clergyman prayed simply for him and left. He returned three hours later to find the boy still alive, but in convulsions. The patient's feet, dead white, were protruding from under the sheet, so the clergyman stood at the foot of the bed and prayed, laying his hands on the boy's feet. "Instantly," he says, "I felt blood pouring down into those feet, and within two seconds he was out of his convulsion." To the surprise of the attending doctors, the boy immediately began to improve in every way, and within a short time had made a complete and uneventful recovery.

Case #85 . . . C. M., age one year. Diagnosis: congenital hip dislocation, one leg shorter than the other. She was placed in a cast in which, according to medical opinion, she would have to remain for at least two years. She was carried to weekly healing services for a period of about a month, her entire body encased in a cast. At the end of this time, her condition had improved to the point where the cast was removed, and she was put into a brace. The healing services were continued for another month, at the end of which time the brace was removed, and she was pronounced by her doctor completely healed.

Case #39 . . . W. K., age 42. Diagnosis: tachycardia (abnormal rapidity of heart action). Patient was sent home from work. For six weeks he alternated between chair and sofa. His wife called minister to lay on hands. Patient was an unbeliever, but finally consented. He lay down on sofa, wife and clergyman kneeling beside him, the latter placing his hand over the patient's heart. Patient began to sweat profusely in pulse point on neck. As healing prayer continued, he felt an instantaneous and terrific pain at the same pulse point in his neck. He was convinced that he had been healed. A visit to his doctor that same night confirmed his belief. His health has since been perfect. The man is no longer an unbeliever.

Case #23 . . . B. R., age about 60. Diagnosis: sinusitis. The patient had suffered a painful sinus condition in the right antrum and frontal sinuses, for which he had been medically treated since the age of twenty-two years. During a particularly acute attack which had kept him up all night, he attended a healing service at the instigation of his family. Before the service ended, he had to blow his nose. The sinus had opened and the pain was gone. The antrum continued to drain freely the remainder of the day. By the next morning, the patient was entirely free from drainage and pain. There has been no recurrence of sinus trouble for more than five years.

Case #75 . . . P. L., age 60. Diagnosis: incurable deafness of right ear. The patient had been deaf for fifteen years.

He attended a healing service to pray for his wife—not himself. He suddenly felt an intense burning in his right ear. His hearing had been instantly restored.

Case #48 . . . L. J., age 62. Diagnosis: incompletely healed fracture, resulting in formation of "false joint." Patient had fallen early in year, injuring both his right knee and his right collarbone, or clavicle. The knee had healed, but clavicle had not. It later developed that the collarbone had been fractured. X-rays revealed that a "false joint" had been formed. Such a condition means that the fracture does not knit: the outer covering of the bone grows over each broken end, and a callous forms around the fractured area. The callous was evident in an inflamed lump, very painful, about the size of a walnut. Patient unable to raise his arm more than a few inches. A scientist, the man was wholly skeptical of spiritual healing, but at the insistence of his wife and son, he attended a service of spiritual healing. During the service he was aware of a strong burning sensation in the area of his shoulder, which he attributed to an over-active "imagination."

Upon his arrival at home after the service, he went in the bathroom to take a shower. Unthinkingly he raised his arm above his head to pull over the shower curtain. He felt quickly for the lump and found that it had disappeared. Since that time, four years ago, he has retained full and normal use of his arm. X-rays taken after the healing reveal the normal condition of right clavicle. (It is not impossible for a false joint to heal naturally, but any normal healing takes a number of weeks, and the condition usually requires surgery, in which the callous is removed, and the ends of the fracture scraped and set.)

Case #29 ... K. S., age 48. Diagnosis: severe brain injury. (Descending medullary paralysis from cerebral concussion, believed by neurologist called in consultation to be a terminal disorder.) Patient was in automobile accident, incurring fracture of leg and collarbone, and severe head injuries. Doctor claimed it most unlikely that she could survive, and "if by some miracle she pulls through, she will be permanently invalided by brain disorder."

She was spiritually healed, and returned to her home within a month, completely well both mentally and physically.

Case #17 ... C. C., age 8. Diagnosis: virus infection of brain and spinal cord. Patient developed high fever. Within twenty-four hours she had lapsed into unconsciousness, and was completely paralyzed from the neck down. On third day she developed convulsions. Her fever rose to 106. Penicillin and other antibiotics were used as well as the customary supportive measures such as intravenous medications, etc. The doctor in charge of the case, as well as all four pediatricians working under his supervision, conceded that it was hopeless.

The mother asked the prayers of various churches in her community and then called in a physician who practiced spiritual healing along with medicine.

He entered the child's room, placed his hands on her, and began to pray. Instantly the convulsions stopped, and she relapsed into what appeared to be a natural sleep. The doctor remained with his hands on the patient for about ten minutes, then left the hospital.

Next morning he stopped by to see the small girl and found her still unconscious, but moving her formerly paralyzed legs in a semi-conscious fashion. Doctor again laid on hands, praying specifically for a healing of the child's legs and arms. On the third day, the child was fully conscious, and had full use of her extremities.

Case #15 ... B. T., age 46. Diagnosis: lobar pneumonia. Patient had fever of 104; antibiotics could not be used due to allergic reaction. At the end of three days, doctors told patient's wife that recovery was extremely doubtful. Clergyman went at once to the hospital to hold healing prayers, and patient immediately lapsed into first natural sleep in three days. Clergyman repeated prayers the next morning, during which the patient dramatically rallied. He made a speedy and uneventful recovery, to the acknowledged surprise of the hospital staff.

Case #69 ... P. B., age 49. Diagnosis: varicose ulcer of leg. Patient had been under medical care for several years, but his condition had continued to worsen until he was virtually incapacitated and suffering intense pain. In 1952, the patient's wife was taken by a friend to her first healing service where she prayed for her husband. That same night, when the patient was unable to sleep from pain, the wife laid her hands gently on his leg and prayed the healing prayer. At once the pain ceased, and the patient slept throughout the night for the first time in many months.

Until this time an unbeliever, the patient went to a healing service with his wife three days later, first protesting that he could not kneel because of his leg. While in the church he found himself on his knees, and was completely healed at the Altar.

Case #18 . . . A. W., age about 60. Diagnosis: bursitis. The patient had suffered from severe bursitis on the right side for three years. Cortisone and other treatment had brought no relief. The affliction then went to the left side where, according to the patient, "from shoulder to fingers it produced the most agonizing pain I have ever felt."

At midnight, his wife called her clergyman, asking that he add his prayers to hers, for her husband's relief. At 12:30 A.M. the patient was peacefully asleep, awakening the next morning with no sign of bursitis. Over a period of four years, there has been no recurrence of the ailment. This case is interesting because of the patient's comment. "As a medical man," he says, "you may know that I had no faith whatsoever in spiritual healing before this happened to me. Now, my own experience plus the many more which have since come to my attention leave me in no doubt as to the actual healing power of God."

Case #94 . . . E. R., age 21. Diagnosis: paralysis of entire left side due to pressure on the brain caused by birth injury. Condition inoperable. Patient was completely cured through spiritual healing. Hers was a gradual healing, occurring over a period of three years.

Case #98 . . . C. S., age 19. Diagnosis: peritonitis. Hospital called patient's parents at midnight to report that he was dying. Clergyman was summoned to give last rites of the Church. The priest entered the boy's room, voicing his assurance that the patient would live. He laid on hands at once, and instantly the boy rallied. The improvement continued. His recovery was rapid and complete.

Case #64 . . . D. N., age 58. Diagnosis: coronary occlusion. Patient suffered coronary attack while on vacation. He was rushed to hospital. While awaiting preparation of oxygen tent, chaplain laid on hands for healing. By the time oxygen was ready, patient did not need it. Cardiogram made directly after attack revealed infarction—badly damaged heart muscle. Attending doctors anticipated a hospital stay of many weeks, followed by months of recuperation at home. Patient received laying-on-of-hands on two succeeding days. Each time discernible improvement followed the rite. Patient was out of the hospital and back at work within ten days. Cardiogram verified healing. Doctors' comment: "Most remarkable recovery."

Case #77 . . . Mrs. W. W., age 36. Diagnosis: cancer of the brain. Condition diagnosed at Walter Reed Hospital and confirmed at Albany Cancer Clinic. Cancer was located towards the back and right side of brain; inoperable. Patient was taking large daily doses of morphine in what proved a futile attempt to relieve unendurable headache. Dismissed from the hospital weighing eighty-four pounds, her life expectancy was estimated at less than one year.

At her husband's instigation, she sought spiritual healing and received an instantaneous cure of headache. She rapidly regained normal weight, and has had no recurrence of pain since that time nearly seven years ago. She has refused to submit to the ordeal of more brain X-rays, but gives every indication of being in excellent health.

It was the multiplicity of cases like these which led me from my planned, rather cursory examination of a few alleged healings into an exhaustive investigative project.

5

Reasons for the Decline of the Healing Ministry

THE RESULTS of my lengthy investigation were, to me, a staggering revelation. There had been many mornings during those months of interviewing and collecting evidence when, upon awakening, I had the uneasy feeling that I must have dreamed up the whole thing.

Now, as I studied my copious notes and filed the evidence, I knew that it was no dream; these "miracles" of physical healing were actually taking place. Even so, the feeling of unreality persisted to some extent. That miracles could be occurring in the middle of the twentieth century just didn't make sense—at least to a skeptical reporter like myself.

Yet it was because I *was* a reporter that I felt impelled to find out the "hows" and "whys"of this phenomenon. My work had trained me to regard facts with a good healthy respect. I now had my facts, and they were indisputable: scores of medically diagnosed cases of congenital and organic disease were, beyond any shadow of doubt, being healed by spiritual means. I had seen numerous such healings taking place, and I now held in my hands the concrete, scientific proof.

My reaction was curious. Intellectually, I was compelled

on the basis of incontrovertible evidence to believe in the validity of these healings. However, emotionally, I was totally unprepared to accept them as direct evidence of God's power. To ascribe what was happening to the intervention of the Holy Spirit seemed to me a conception at once childish and neurotic. And yet, I puzzled, the men and women whom I had seen walk in dignity and faith to the Altar for the laying-on-of-hands—those many whom I had interviewed at length after their healings—seemed neither childishly gullible nor neurotic, but well-balanced, intelligent persons, quietly certain of the demonstrable power of a living God.

I couldn't figure it out, but I certainly wasn't prepared at the time to go along with them in their conviction. All I could do was to acknowledge that a great outside force had, apparently, been unleashed. A hitherto unknown law was obviously in effect. The answer would, I was sure, be eventually found in science.

In any event, the thing was incredibly exciting. With imagination fired and curiosity whetted, I was determined to get to the bottom of this fabulous story, regardless of the months of research it might involve. I believed I had stumbled on a new and startling "invention." With the excitement of a Columbus discovering America, I was sure that I, too, had discovered a new scientific continent.

It was a chance meeting with Bishop Austin Pardue which was to direct me to the next phase of my research. It was he who gave me the key, when, in answer to my comments on the "new" phenomenon being demonstrated in the Pittsburgh Diocese, the Bishop assured me that the healings taking place were in no sense a "new invention," but the result of a revitalization of one of the oldest and greatest ministries of the Church.

As we parted on the steps of Trinity Cathedral, I asked myself two pertinent questions: What had happened to this so-called great ministry that it should have lain dormant for centuries? Had such a healing ministry ever indeed existed?

I figured that these were two questions which could be answered with a minimum of work. The source material available would surely be scant and far from authentic. Thus, with a modicum of boredom and with complete skepticism, I undertook a weekend of reading about healing in the Early Church. That weekend was to stretch into many months of the most absorbing and productive research I had ever undertaken, for, to my amazement, a totally unsuspected wealth of relevant and authoritative material confronted me.

Long before I began my research, I had been aware of so-called "faith" cures. I knew that from primitive man with his good luck charms, up to our recent "medicine man" with his bottle of sugared water "guaranteed" to cure everything from corns to cancer, man has sought relief from his ailments by other than scientific means.

Healing through the mind was certainly nothing new. There is ample evidence that it began twenty thousand years before Christ, and it has continued in different and pseudo-scientific versions through Mesmer and Coué, hypnotism and suggestibility, psychoanalysis and religionism. We know the value of these methods in healing psychosomatic disease. But when did hypnotism ever cure a cancer—or Couéism, with the incantation "every day in every way, I'm getting better and better," ever heal a lung lesion?

Psychoanalysis has proved beneficial in certain cases, and the value of religion as a psychotherapeutic aid has long been recognized by many psychiatrists. Indeed, Dr. C. G. Jung, eminent psychologist and physician, has stated: "It is safe to say that among all my patients in the second half of life, every one of them fell ill because he had lost that which the living religions of every age have given to their followers. None of them has really been healed who did not regain his religious outlook."

But wonderful as are psychological cures, it was actual physical healings of organic disease which interested me. What part had the Church ever played in healing purely physical ailments? I soon found out.

The great healing ministry of the Christian Church actually began in the New Testament with the book of Acts, which records some thirteen clear-cut physical healings after Christ's Ascension. "By the hands of the apostles were many signs and wonders wrought among the people" (Acts 5:12).

However, we are not dependent on the word of mouth "fables," as some term them, of the New Testament. Through the prolific writings of the early Christians known as the Fathers of the Church, we are able to follow closely, by means of eye-witness reports, the history of healing in the Church through the first three centuries after Christ. During these three hundred years, the healing of the body was a vitally important function of the Church, discharged with conspicuous success.

The writings of the early Church Fathers upon which the evidence is based are clearly not the emotional outpourings of religious fanatics. They are, rather, meticulous records, prepared by intelligent and highly educated men, fully aware that their work would probably be exposed to merciless investigation by the Roman authorities.

Irenaeus, Tertullian, Origen, Justin Martyr, and many others, too numerous to mention, all great intellectuals of their time, have marshalled impressive evidence regarding spiritual healing in the Early Church.

Tertullian, a Christian convert, later to become one of Rome's great theologians, cites numerous instances of physical healings in his writings. In his *On the Flesh of Christ*, written about A.D. 200, he tells specifically of healings of leprosy, blindness, and palsy, and makes frequent mention of the raising of the dead.

Origen, teacher, writer, and considered one of the greatest thinkers of the early Christian Church, offers convincing evidence of the prevalence of physical healings, in his work *Against Celsus*, written in the third century.

One of the greatest single sources of information concerning miraculous healings lies in a treatise called *Against Heresies*, written about A.D. 170 by Irenaeus, eminent Greek churchman in Gaul. In this work, the author deals at length and in detail with the healings, which "occur daily," of blindness, leprosy, deafness, etc., as well as the raising of the dead: "the entire Church entreating that boon with much fasting and prayer . . . Those who are in truth His disciples, receiving Grace from Him, do in His Name, perform miracles."

"And one is cured, receiving healing by faith; and the dead is raised up in consequence of the power of one believing that he would be raised," says Clement of Alexandria in the first century.

"In the Name of Jesus Christ, our Christian men have healed and do heal," exclaims Justin Martyr in the second century.

"The Name of Jesus repels demons and takes away disease," states Origen in the third century.

We are assured again and again that through prayer, implemented by the laying-on-of-hands, holy anointing, exorcism in the Name of Jesus Christ, and the sign of the Cross, these healings were being received by the faithful— healings so numerous and so miraculous that even the Roman authorities were obliged to confirm them.

Throughout all the writings of the early Christians runs the same recurrent theme: no disease can remain impervious to the power of the Holy Spirit; for all who believe on Him, this power is abundantly available.

But can we really believe the writings of these early Christian teachers, philosophers, and theologians, or is the evidence they present the fabrication of over-stimulated imaginations, the product of over-zealous hearts?

After a concentrated study of their reasoned and schol-arly expositions, I can only reasonably conclude that such unanimity of experience as reported by so many honest and intelligent men, at different times and from different places, constitutes reliable historical evidence, fully as worthy of credence as the data compiled by any other historians, upon whose written word we have necessarily based our total knowledge of history.

It is abundantly clear that the great healing ministry of Christ was, in the post-apostolic days, and according to His command, channelled and manifested through His Body, the Church. The power of God was a living reality to thousands of the faithful. Eyewitness accounts, including those of Ignatius, martyred in A.D. 117, relate numerous instances of those martyrs who were thrown to the wild beasts and emerged unscathed; of those persecuted who en-dured the most unspeakable torture, yet felt no pain, pro-tected as they were by the invulnerable armour of their faith in the near Presence of their Lord.

What happened, then, to this great healing and protective power? Why, at the beginning of the fourth century, did St. Augustine refer to miracles as being most unusual, and apparently becoming increasingly rare?

The explanation would seem to lie in three primary factors: controversy within the Church which lessened her spiritual power; the conflict between science and religion, which was already under way by the fourth century; and finally, the most fundamental reason of all, a diminishment of faith.

The once united Church was now split by controversy and infiltrated by heretics. No longer was it standing steadfast and inviolable upon the Rock of Peter, but much as today, it was floundering in a morass of conflicting opinion. The once invincible power of prayer—invincible because of unity of faith—had been decimated by divided opinion. The historic faith was even then being invaded by the liberalism which has jeopardized, ever since, the cause of Christianity. The splitting of doctrinal hairs had already begun —a practice which, down to the present time, continues to weaken the Church.

The quiet harbor, sought and previously found by the Holy Spirit, had been transformed into a mad maelstrom of human conflict—an atmosphere hardly conducive to spiritual healing.

The problem of the lost faith was a vicious circle. The power of healing was lost, in the last analysis, because of lack of faith. Yet, conversely, as the healing ministry declined, so, in direct proportion, did the remaining faith in miracles diminish.

Faith is, of course, always a tenuous, ephemeral thing, and never easy. Even for the Disciples, with their Master beside them, it was hard to retain. Small wonder, then, that gradually, almost imperceptibly, the glowing and dynamic faith left by Christ and replenished by the Holy Spirit should have dwindled, particularly as the dawn of science was breaking.

For already science was beginning to come into its own. A recalcitrant and unyielding Church, refusing to relinquish her ministry of healing, which was even then largely impotent, made inevitable the schism between religion and science which has remained for sixteen hundred years.

By rationalizing her own lost power to heal as evidence of God's will that humanity should suffer; by refusing to accept the proven scientific truths pertaining to disease and its prevention; by obstructing science at every turn, the Church unwittingly began the conflict which is only now beginning to be resolved.

The Church's attitude wreaked havoc, for not only did she hopelessly antagonize science, but her actions further weakened the faith of her own members. Christians saw with their own eyes that medicine healed where the Church failed. They sought drugs to the exclusion of God. The age of materialism was on its way.

Not realizing that God was responsible for *all* healing, regardless of method, the laymen's allegiance began, at first subtly and then with increasing vigor, to be transferred from the Church to science, from God to drugs, whose efficacy was tangible, concrete, and incontestable. Incidentally, taking a pill was easier then, as it is now, than the faith and true repentance necessary for spiritual healing.

Science, then man himself, became the object of worship. The faith of the Christian world was gradually being placed in man's brain rather than in its Creator. Here were sown the first seeds of Humanism.

For those first three hundred years, the Church had obeyed our Lord's command to heal. Those were the years of persecution, when the faith of the Christians flamed; when the Church was indeed Christ's Body, moved, led, and inspired by Him, and filled with His Spirit—His promised legacy to mankind.

Those were the years when the Church, uncorrupted by material prosperity, unconcerned with political ambition, undivided by schism, successfully obeyed our Lord's command.

Those were the days of which Irenaeus wrote, "None who believe in Christ and call upon His Name remain unhealed."

Those were the days when Tertullian wrote that not only was all disease healed, but the dead were frequently raised.

Those were the days when the certainty of cure was never questioned; when healing was received in expectant faith; when the Church considered it a great sin to fail to heal.

The dark ages of the Church began in the fourth century, when, no longer persecuted, the dynamic faith of the Christian degenerated into prosaic lip-service; when, corrupted by prosperity, degraded by political ambition, divided by schism and weakened by moral laxity, the Church gradually lost her power to heal. Her faithlessness not only drove her members into the arms of the medical profession, but drove the profession of medicine out of the monasteries where it was first largely developed.

The age of heresy was under way, the heresy that God wills disease and sends it as a means of punishment for his recalcitrant children.

Pondering the results of these conclusions, it began to seem for the first time credible that the healings taking place today might mean the renascence of the ancient and powerful healing ministry.

Could it be, I dared to ask myself, that these miracles were not merely a scientific phenomenon, but instead, a direct and purposeful manifestation of the power of God?

I was awed at the thought, and frankly, considerably embarrassed to be harboring it. I could visualize all too well the jibes of my fellow reporters, who, like myself, were not exactly renowned for their spiritual proclivities! I knew well enough that, were they to guess the direction of my thoughts at this time, they would have me slated for a quick trip to the nearest mental hospital!

Well—I wasn't worried about my sanity because I wasn't quite ready as yet to go all the way with the Holy Spirit theory. However, very cautiously, and strictly to myself, I had to admit the possibility that those who believed might have some logical basis for their faith.

6

The Difference Between Faith Healing and Spiritual Healing

IT IS a strange human perversity that while we seek, often with near-desperation, demonstrable evidence that God exists, we do everything in our power to discredit that evidence when confronted by it.

We are, generally speaking, willing to render unto Caesar that which is Caesar's, but when it comes to God, that's a different matter. We will fight to the last ditch against rendering unto Him that which is His. I was no exception. No agnostic ever tried more assiduously than I to disprove what seemed to me the fantastic notion that God was miraculously healing the sick.

Because I believe that my own reactions to the question of spiritual healing were in many respects typical, I would like to detail here a few of the "reasoned" arguments I propounded in my effort to explain away the phenomenon.

I founded my case primarily on the premise that "miracles" are not admissible in the world of science. With no scientific basis for their existence, they therefore could not be. It was some time before I realized that in my anxiety to present a valid case against God, I had ended by disavowing that very science in which I had placed my faith.

This is what I mean: Take the case of a man dying of

pneumonia. He is given a shot of penicillin, and recovers His friends and relatives exclaim, "Thank heaven for penicillin! It saved his life!" They don't lie awake nights thinking up reasons why penicillin had nothing whatsoever to do with his recovery.

"Of course not," you retort, as did I. "The effectiveness of penicillin against pneumonia has been *scientifically* proved."

Exactly. But take, then, the case of a man dying of an inoperable cancer. His ailment has been diagnosed by modern scientific laboratory procedure—the accuracy of which has been as incontestably proved as has the efficacy of penicillin against pneumonia. The cancer victim is spiritually healed and what happens? When confronted with the fact of his recovery, our faith in science inexplicably flies out the window. We are suddenly and unalterably convinced that X-rays lie, and microscopes deceive. "Wrong diagnosis," we shout. And for a long time my voice led all the rest.

Now there is no doubt that a particular individual may have received a wrong diagnosis. There is always a human margin of error, no matter what the actual scientific method. X-rays can be misread and the microscopic analysis of tissue can be misinterpreted, but only in isolated instances —not time after time. As the evidence mounted, bearing witness to the fact that an extremely large number of scientifically diagnosed incurables were being healed, it eventually seemed to me that there was only one of two logical conclusions to be derived from the facts: either these so-called incurable cases were being healed by an outside force, or an appalling number of doctors are charlatans, and modern diagnostic techniques are totally worthless.

I chose the former explanation as the more rational. I

simply do not believe that doctors in general are criminally incompetent, nor the procedures they use entirely untrustworthy.

In recognition, then, of the illogical conclusions to which my "logical" reasoning had led me, I was forced, in honesty, to repudiate the "wrong diagnosis" theory.

As my investigations progressed, my carefully manufactured explanations, calculated to deny God's healing power, fell by the wayside.

I had, of course, toyed briefly with the "imaginary" illness idea. Surely, I argued, the ailments for which cures had been claimed were purely imaginary. Investigation revealed, however, that although a few suffering from apparently non-existent ailments had claimed "cures," these were distinctly in the minority. The vast majority, according to scientific evidence, have suffered disabilities which were indeed real.

A 40-year-old woman, who a reputable doctor had testified had no eardrums, suddenly hears for the first time in her life. Had she, with no eardrums, merely *imagined* that she could not hear before?

A blind man suddenly regains his sight. It is a matter of public record that, twenty years before, his cornea had been destroyed by a splinter of molten steel. Had he merely *imagined* that he could not see before?

Scores of similar cases caused my theory of imaginary illness to topple.

Next I explored the "previous medical treatment" theory. I knew that most of the cases seeking spiritual healing had been medically treated for years, apparently without result. Could it be, I wondered, that those patients who thought themselves "spiritually" healed were in reality experiencing a delayed response to their earlier medical care? Within a month I was forced to discard this hypothesis as invalid. There is no doubt that such a thing might happen occasionally, but it just didn't make sense that time after time the "response," delayed for years, should suddenly occur in the middle of a healing service.

By this time, it seemed virtually impossible to explain away the healings I was witnessing. Nonetheless, I was a long way from accepting the Holy Spirit explanation so glibly offered by those healed.

The answer, I told myself, *must* lie in science—and here I was right back where I had started months before. By this time I was convinced that a higher scientific law, of which we were ignorant, was in operation. What was happening must be some sort of scientific phenomenon.

With this explanation I was more or less content—until I began to take note of what was happening to the *lives* of those who had been healed.

A man, who as the result of a hopeless spinal injury was doomed to a life of complete invalidism and intolerable pain, was healed instantly. Resuming his former job at a mill, he promptly started weekly prayer meetings with his working companions.

A man, who for years had gambled away his earnings and abused his family, felt the Lord's healing touch. He turned to God, gave up gambling, and is now a model husband and father.

A wealthy, spoiled woman, having felt the healing power, now gives unstintingly of her wealth and time and energy to assist in setting up healing missions all over the country.

And there are scores of run-of-the-mine people, like you

and me, neither particularly good nor particularly bad, who, having been healed, work unceasingly with grateful hearts and eager hands so that others, too, may know what they have discovered.

Was all of this coincidence? No, for I found that the inspiring stories of changed lives are as many as those healed.

After talking to over a hundred of these people, I began, at last, to comprehend the true significance of their healings. It gradually became clear to me that spiritual healing, achieved through faith in God and in the promises of His Son, Jesus Christ, has one purpose only—the soul's salvation. The physical healing was incidental—only a small part of the healing of the whole man. Wonderful and dramatic as it is that the blind see, and the deaf hear, and the crippled take up their beds and walk, it was far *more* wonderful, and infinitely more exciting, to witness the spiritual regeneration which seemed inevitably to follow the healing of the body.

Could the operation of a higher scientific law, I asked myself, induce a spiritual rebirth? The answer seemed to me an unequivocal "no." And with that answer, I became aware, for the first time, of the basic and unassailable difference between faith cures and spiritual healing.

The *obvious* difference between faith cures and spiritual healing had long been clear. I knew, for example, that the "faith" a patient has in his doctor can constitute a life-saving factor in his recovery. I knew that the "faith" an individual may have in a talisman, or his belief in the curative powers of some substance, even if it is only sugared water, can be beneficial to many, *if* those individuals are extremely susceptible to suggestion, and *if* they have no congenital or organic physical ailment.

I knew, on the other hand, that spiritual healing knows no limitations and accepts no boundaries, but until now, I had overlooked the most important element of difference between the two. No cure of a psychosomatic ailment, wrought through "faith" in a material gadget, has ever resulted in any *spiritual* change or growth.

The functional heart patient often experiences improvement when he goes to a new doctor in whom he has more "faith." Will this "cure" lead to spiritual growth? No, and if the heart is organically diseased, the patient will soon lapse into his former condition.

A patient suffering nervous indigestion can be improved by taking a harmless patent medicine which she is sure will cure her because it helped a friend of hers. Will this "cure" lead to conversion? No, and if the nervous indigestion is, in reality, cancer of the stomach, any improvement will be wholly imaginary.

A patient with nervous headaches can be "cured" by taking a sugar pill, if his "faith" in the curative power of the pill is sufficiently great. Will this "cure" result in a regenerated life? No, and if his headaches are the result, not of tension, but of a brain tumor, the sugar pills won't help for long.

The fact is, there are no records extant which indicate that faith in anything but Jesus Christ ever healed actual organic disease or true congenital defects—or a sick soul.

As far back as the third century, when healing was still a vital part of the Church's ministry, heretics of the day claimed miraculous healings which equalled those of the Christians. Investigation by Irenaeus, outstanding scholar of his time, indicated that the claims were fraudulent. In his *Against Heresies*, he lists those whom *only Christians* could cure. Among them are the blind, the deaf, and the crippled since birth—all with what we now call congenital ailments.

And so it seems to be today. Can faith in a patent medicine restore health to a cancer-ridden victim? Can faith in a doctor create a new eardrum? Can faith in a talisman fuse a bone? And, infinitely more important, can faith in anything but Jesus Christ save the soul?

I found the answer in an exhaustive study of relevant material; and I found it, above all, in my observation of those who have been spiritually healed.

For nearly two thousand years, restoration of the spirit as well as the body has been indigenous to Christian healing. Again and again we read in the New Testament that those who were healed by our Lord were affected spiritually as well as physically. "All men glorified God for that which was done" (Acts 4:21).

The changed lives and glowing faces of those I have seen healed are surely the outward and visible signs of the inward and spiritual grace with which they have been so abundantly endued. Their healthy bodies and regenerate lives, dedicated to the glory of God, would seem to bear indisputable witness to the fact that God lives.

Those who have felt the healing power can never again be the same. Even a casual observer is aware that, somehow, they are different. An inner radiance seems to flood their faces, often lending to their features an almost luminous appearance. It was my noting of this phenomenon, again and again, which was to lead me to believe.

Not long ago I had dinner with an executive of a large corporation whom I knew to be a free thinker. During the course of the meal, a man healed of lung cancer, whom I had interviewed some months before, stopped at our table. I introduced him to my friend, we spoke briefly, and the man went on his way.

I turned back to my dinner companion to resume our interrupted conversation, and I saw his glance follow the man to the door. He turned to me with a look of bewilderment on his face. "Who *was* that man?" he asked. "Did you notice that strange glow he had, or am I crazy?"

I explained briefly—and for over an hour he bombarded me with eager questions. As we paid our bill, he remarked: "You know, I've always believed you were an honest reporter, but frankly, if I hadn't just seen that man, I'd be certain you had a screw loose. *Having* seen him, I'm not surprised at anything you've told me. Now don't get me wrong. I don't believe in this sort of thing, but that man has experienced something I don't know anything about. I'm just curious enough to want to learn more. How about dinner next week?"

As I look back now, I see that the first real assault on my own unbelief began on the day I was forced to concede that a great outside healing power was at work. Conferences with doctors, innumerable interviews, and a long and arduous study of the medical histories of hopelessly broken bodies, now fully restored, had left me no alternative explanation.

I was not able to define that power until I realized that the healings extended far beyond the realm of the purely physical. The death knell of my skepticism was to sound when I grasped their true significance. It was then that I became convinced that the phenomenon was of God.

I, of course, do not *know*—perhaps no one who is only an observer *can* know—whether these miraculous healings are actually a direct and personal manifestation of the Holy Spirit. I can only state that in the opinion of an unbiased reporter honestly seeking the truth, the cumulative evidence indicates that this healing power is not an unknown scientific law called, for some mysterious reason, into startling operation. It is my deep conviction, based on massive evidence and personal observation, that it is the direct intervention of the Holy Spirit in our lives—the evidence we have long sought of a living God.

7

Credo

BY THIS time, I was committed to far more than a belief in spiritual healing. I was irrevocably committed to the doctrine of Jesus Christ as proclaimed by the Church.

"By their fruits ye shall know them." The Church was demonstrating for me and for many the inalienable truth of the faith it promulgated.

Had I been an agnostic before? I certainly had not considered myself such. If anyone had asked me whether I believed in God, I would have replied, "Yes." If anyone had asked whether I were a Christian, my answer would likewise have been in the affirmative. I see now that I would unwittingly have been committing perjury, for the truth of the matter was that, to me, God was merely a convenient abstraction, while Christianity consisted of abiding, in so far as was practicable, by the Golden Rule. Oh, I had searched once, years ago, for a more satisfactory, a more personal concept, but I had not found it. I had long since grown weary of the search. "Seek and ye shall find" had lost any personal significance. It was a well-phrased slogan, applicable to everything except religion.

For some, faith comes easily. In my ignorance, I had thought that those who could obey His command, "Follow thou me," without question, were unthinking, rather stupid people. I know now that they are the inestimably blessed.

For others, like myself, the acquisition of real faith is a difficult and often acutely painful process: a war of attrition between mind and heart. But if years ago I had managed to rationalize myself out of belief, I was, through my interest in spiritual healing, to reason myself into faith.

I was neither healed of any physical disability nor was I, in the usual sense, converted. But in seeking an explanation for the phenomenon of non-medical healings, I was forced into an analysis of Christianity.

I had long considered the basic, Church-held concept of Jesus Christ impossible to believe, and then I stumbled, as I think now, with purpose, onto the phenomenon of spiritual healing. If these miracles of healing occurring today were possible, then, obviously, *anything* was possible, or to put it another way, from the Virgin Birth through the Resurrection and Ascension, the entire concept of Christianity was intellectually impossible. So were the present miracles of healing. The words of Tertullian flashed through my mind: "It is certain *because* it is impossible." I knew now exactly what he meant.

The whole thing fell into place like the pieces of a jigsaw puzzle when I finally selected what seemed to me the more logical of two basic premises: either Christianity is the greatest hoax ever perpetrated upon mankind or the great tenets of the Christian faith are eternal and unchangeable truth—not a matter of mere mores.

I could find no evidence to substantiate the first contention. I believe that there is demonstrable proof of the validity of the latter premise. On this I base my own *personal* case for Christianity.

When Christ's commandments are obeyed, the results are as He promised. The faithful have long known this. I did not believe it until I saw the evidence offered in the ministry of spiritual healing. "Whatsoever ye shall ask in my name, that will I do" (John 14:13). "According to your faith be it unto you" (Matthew 9:29). "If thou canst believe, all things are possible" (Mark 9:23).

Again and again He makes like promises, and again and again I have seen these promises fulfilled when they are claimed. As Dr. R. B. Bell, founder of the Life Abundant Movement, states: "All power was promised to the followers of Jesus Christ if they observed His rules and followed His commandments exactly as He issued them. The Christian churches must understand that the Gospel is the teaching, words and sermons of Jesus as He propounded them—and not what anyone else *says* about them —not even the Apostles."

If we choose that which we want to believe and eschew the rest; if we individually select what we consider is currently applicable and what is not; if we assume personal authority over the Gospel facts, then we are superseding Christ's authority by our own. We are making of Christianity a hollow travesty. We are living by a pagan superstition, rather than by the inviolable truths of a great faith.

I had called myself a Christian, but I had never taken the time nor trouble to decipher either the meaning or the implication of Christianity. Perhaps this was because I was guilty of the cowardice which I think the modern Church has fostered—the fear of believing too much, which results so often in believing nothing at all. Perhaps it was because at that time I could not or would not hurdle the stumbling blocks inherent in the Gospels—stumbling blocks caused not by the things I didn't understand in the New Testament, but by the things I *did* understand but didn't want to believe.

I laughed off, for instance, the doctrine of Original Sin. "He is the propitiation for our sins." *What* sins? *I* hadn't done anything to be ashamed of! Then one day it occurred to me that if I discarded this premise, I must discard, in His entirety, Jesus Christ. Unless Original Sin were presupposed, Christ's mission on earth to redeem and save mankind was a meaningless farce. If man were without sin, he had no need of a redeemer, having nothing from which to be redeemed. In this case, the doctrine of the Atonement was necessarily a wholly invalid figment of man's imagination.

I denied His Divinity. After all, this is an enlightened age. The supernatural is intellectually unacceptable. Then I realized that either He was the Son of God as He claimed, or a prodigious liar and dangerous psychopath, whose teachings should be relegated to obscurity as the ravings of a madman.

I repudiated His miracles, obviously mere fantasy: myths perpetrated by over-enthusiastic Gospel writers. I gradually awoke to the fact that if I denied those miracles, I must, in consistency, deny the Resurrection. And just where does that leave Christianity?

To take literally His origin, destiny, and even most of His teaching was stretching credulity too far. I would not go beyond my admission that He was a good Man and a great Teacher, that is, if one had the native intelligence to differentiate in what He taught between what was practical and what was hopeless idealism, obviously not intended for present-day living.

Turn the other cheek? Give him who had stolen my coat, my cloak also? Surely no one in his right mind could take this sort of "teaching" seriously!

Oh, I believed *parts* of the New Testament. I was heartily in favor of spreading "Christianity." It was a fine ethical and moral code. I was ready to go along with Jesus' command to preach the Kingdom of God, but I took it upon myself (supported by most of the churches) to peremptorily dismiss the second portion of the command, to "heal the sick" (Luke 9:2).

"Go ye into all the world and preach the gospel to every living creature" seemed a pretty good idea, but just let's forget the rest of it, when He said, in no uncertain terms: "And these signs shall follow them that believe . . . they shall cast out devils; . . . they shall lay hands on the sick, and they shall recover" (Mark 16:17, 18).

It took a long time, but eventually I became convinced of the fallacy of this sort of unauthoritative selective belief. It seemed to me that wherever it was indulged in, spiritual strength was dissipated and the cause of Christianity weakened.

They say that faith is more a matter of the heart than of the mind, and this is essentially true. But there is a vast difference between *belief* and *faith,* even though the one almost invariably follows the other.

Belief is the mind's acceptance, and faith is the heart's receiving. My heart was to remain locked until my mind could accept Him.

My faith came, not as a sudden and dramatic conversion, but by means of a rather torturously-arrived-at intellectual conviction—a conviction predicated on the fact that, to me, Christianity made good sense, but to derive the sense from it, I must believe what Christ taught in its entirety, or I must believe none of it. Christianity is not a myth. It is an historical and clearly definitive religion; there are no half-way measures. I feel that neither I, a layman, nor any theologian, however learned, can choose at random and select without authority that which is convenient for the one to believe and interesting for the other to teach. If we take it upon ourselves to do so, we are distorting Christianity into a man-created code of half-truths, and the step from a half-truth to a lie is notoriously short.

In my opinion, if we casually overlook, "interpret" away, or attempt to make more palatable the difficult teachings of our Lord, we are degrading Christianity into a chaotic and untrustworthy cult. To me, either the whole thing is true, or the whole thing is false. You make your choice. I made mine, not long ago, on the basis of the results of true Christian faith as I saw them first, in spiritual healing of the body, and as I have recognized them since, in spiritual healing of the soul.

My mind's acceptance proved the key which was to open my heart to full faith. As He entered in, I was suddenly aware that He had been standing there all the time, quite able to enter, but waiting for me to unlock the door myself. With my mind, I had been able to "look through a glass, darkly." With my heart, I saw.

I repudiated my background, which for so long had conditioned me against literal Christianity. I reversed my former beliefs and corrected my former misapprehensions, such as the one that religion was for the weak. I knew now that a man's strength can be computed by the degree to which he depends on God while his courage can be determined by the extent to which he dares to claim Christ's promises.

I was ready at last to confess a living God and His only begotten Son, Jesus Christ, who was sent to redeem the world.

I believe that through spiritual healing, He has renewed for us the means of faith.

I believe that on love, repentance, and faith hangs the law of salvation.

I believe in our Lord's revelation of a merciful God, who wills neither sin nor disease. Therefore, in order to reconcile this concept of a merciful God and a suffering world, I must believe in the very real powers of evil (the devil, if you like) which are constantly working against God's will in the world.

In stretching forth His hand to heal our souls of sin and our bodies of disease, I believe that He has given us complete assurance of His ultimate victory over evil. Our faith in Him is at once His strongest weapon and our impenetrable armour.

"He that believeth and is baptized, shall be saved; but he that believeth not shall be damned" (Mark 16:16).

I believe that He meant what He said and that no amount of "interpretation" can palliate His commanded mission to His Church: "Preach ye the Kingdom of God—and heal the sick."

8

Implications of the Revival of the Healing Ministry

WE HAVE assumed that spiritual healing flourished during the first few centuries after Christ because the Church then was a truly spiritual body, unweakened by schism and uncorrupted by secularism. Why, then, in an age where worldliness supersedes the spiritual, when, for millions, humanism has become a religion with materialism its creed and science its god, should there be a dramatic renascence of spiritual healing?

Obviously, any answer to this question must be conjectural, but I believe at least part of the answer lies in humanity's desperate need. By providing a spiritually starving world with the food for which it hungers, God, as surely as He did nearly two thousand years ago, has offered His people the sustenance without which they have been perishing. In giving us the tangible and demonstrable evidence that He still lives, He has restored to us the inestimable gift of true and active faith.

He has placed in the hands of His Body, the Church, a great spiritual power which is revitalizing the saving faith of Christians all over the world. He has handed to a jeopardized Christianity the one weapon before which Communism must go down in total defeat—a massed, living faith in Jesus Christ.

Man is born with a compulsive need for religion. He will create one if he hasn't any; and the one that comes most naturally is humanism. None of us finds it very difficult to worship fervently at the altar of our own achievement. But there comes a time, both individually and corporately, when we are forced to turn to something above and beyond ourselves. Such a time has come now, not on an individual, not on a national, but on a world-wide basis.

The highest church membership (but not attendance!) in history and the mushrooming of multitudinous sects, attracting thirty million followers, attest to the fact that man is starving for God.

He has split the atom and made possible his own extermination on a world-wide scale. He sees the world threatened by the anti-Christ of Communism. He is apprehensive as he has never been before. Weak in faith, but strong in desire, he has turned to a God which he hopes exists, with the cry, "Give me a light that I may find my way into the unknown."

Clear and strong has come the answer. "Put your hands in mine, and that shall be to you better than a light and safer than a known way." And that there shall be no confusion, God, through His great healing power, has held out His hand to us and made it visible to all who will turn their heads to see.

Man has sought evidence of a living God since the world began, but never with the avidity with which he seeks it now. So God has performed another miracle, the greatest miracle of all time, except that of Jesus Christ. He has given us the evidence. As more and more of us see and recognize the source of spiritual healing, the faith of the world is being reborn.

Although the revitalization of the healing ministry is

very recent and has not as yet been universally adopted as a compulsory part of church practice, its effect and influence have been both impressive and profound. Already the pale, passive belief of thousands of Christians, far beyond the confines of any one parish, church, or nation, has been galvanized into an active and dynamic faith. Christianity, for too long and for too many a mere code of ethics, is becoming once more the flaming force it used to be, and must become again if the world is to be saved from itself.

The Church, with God's help, has successfully met her greatest challenge. Sometimes, over the past few years, appearing to be the Church Hesitant, she has today, as the source of a limitless spiritual power, become again the Church Militant. She is proclaiming in loud, firm tones her thrilling message of complete conviction—that God lives. She is *demonstrating* the immutable truth she holds, through her ministry of spiritual healing.

Miracles of physical healing today, as they did centuries ago, evoke worship and serve to quicken the faith of men everywhere. Jesus did not perform His miracles as acts of "magic" to prove that He was the Son of God. He offered them as evidence of God's love and compassion. Nevertheless, the Gospels reveal a close and vital connection between His healings and His preaching. He never underestimated the psychological value of the former. You may remember that when two of John the Baptist's disciples came to Him and asked, "Art thou he that should come?" Jesus was quick to answer, "Go and show John again those things which ye do hear and see: the blind receive their sight, and the lame walk, the lepers are cleansed, and the deaf hear . . ." (Matthew 11:3-5).

People living two thousand years ago were much the

same as people living today. A few may have gathered to hear Jesus, the Preacher, for the good of their souls, but the crowds formed in curiosity to see Christ, the Miracle Worker, and many among them came in hope and faith that they would be healed.

When the healings occurred, the people at large were profoundly impressed. As the people of Galilee said, "He hath done all things well. He maketh both the deaf and dumb to speak." The miracles then, as they do today, played a large part in inducing the populace to listen with eager minds and receptive hearts to His message. They offered proof of the validity of our Lord's revelation of a compassionate God, who willed neither disease nor evil in any form.

Again and again, we read in the Acts how spiritual healing, as a *visible* sign of God's love and power, turned people to the Lord. "In the name of Jesus Christ of Nazareth, rise up and walk," said St. Peter to the lame beggar. "And he took him by the right hand and lifted him up: and immediately his feet and ankle bones received strength . . . And all the people saw him walking and praising God" (Acts 3:6, 7, 9). And, subsequently, "many of them which heard the word believed; and the number of men was about five thousand" (Acts 4:4).

And so it is today. Countless people who come to see, and perhaps to scoff, remain to pray and hear the message.

I have seen scores of men and women who have not been inside a church for twenty years return to His house, and grow strong in faith as they witness God's healing power at work.

I have seen numerous unbelievers brought to God by the witness of those healed.

I have seen the electrified faith and spiritual growth of hundreds of churchgoers, as they became aware of a power they never knew existed.

Through the revival of this great spiritual power, God has answered the prayers of the faithful and the hopes of the unchurched. He has made us conscious of His Presence as He never has before. He has literally touched our eyes that we might see Him. He has actually opened our ears that we might hear His voice. Above all, He has entered our hearts that we might know His love.

Those clergymen who administer spiritual healing report that it is the greatest of all their spiritual experiences. The rector of a large city church puts it this way: "My whole life has changed since I undertook the healing ministry. I have a new and tremendously exciting sense of the reality of God."

Another minister says: "I cannot explain it, but the Lord's Presence is never so real or so near as during the laying-on-of-hands."

For me and for many others, this has proved true. It was when I knelt before the Altar to receive Holy Communion immediately followed by the laying-on-of-hands, that I first felt His Presence. This was when my heart accepted Him in faith, as my mind had already accepted Him in belief.

The benefits of spiritual healing are not limited to those who are seeking physical healing, nor are they confined to those who are actually cured of bodily ailments. Those whose bodies have not been healed have received, time and again, the far more important healing of their souls. Touched by the Holy Spirit, they have turned from the

Altar to walk into a new and inspired life. Thousands are being brought to God today, not because they themselves have been physically healed, but because, aware of His great healing power, they at last *know* that God is.

This is why to me, a layman, the ministry of healing is one of the most important, and certainly the most dynamic and exciting, ministries of the Church. No longer is the existence of God a nebulous hope to us of little faith. He is now a reality.

I have not forgotten that "faith is the substance of things hoped for, the evidence of things unseen." But I remember, also, that when Jesus appeared to His Disciples, He said: "Peace be unto you. And when he had so said, he *shewed* unto them his hands and his side. *Then* were the disciples glad, when they saw the Lord" (John 20:19, 20).

I recall, also, that when Thomas expressed his doubt, our Lord said to him: "Reach hither thy finger and behold my hands; and reach hither thy hand, and thrust it into my side: and be not faithless, but believing" (John 20:27).

Then Jesus was to say: "Thomas, because thou hast seen me, thou hast believed: blessed are they that have not seen, and yet have believed" (John 20:29). A mild rebuke, but our Lord understood the difficulties of belief. He offered, not only to Thomas, but to *all* the Disciples, the irrefutable evidence of His identity.

He did not appear to the Scribes and Pharisees and Roman authorities. He came only to those who had the desire, even though the inability, to believe. So He comes today.

Jesus has done no less for us than for His Disciples. He has rewarded us, not according to our merit, but according to our need. He has given us proof, through the healing power, that He lives—proof as certain as the touch of the nail-scarred hands, and as incontestable as the sight of His wounded side.

To all seeking hearts He gives the evidence of His existence. He will not force into belief, by "signs," the Scribes and Pharisees. He will not replace *faith* with absolute knowledge, for faith is an essential and integral part of the God-man relationship. It is the bridge which connects us with God. It is the stairway which, on the steps of repentance, leads to His throne. There is no other way.

Today's miracles of healing, both spiritual and physical, signify the greatest revival of spiritual power the Church has known since the apostolic days. She is again the promulgator of that vibrant and expectant faith which can move mountains.

The clearly perceptible spiritual growth and influence of those churches which have revitalized the healing ministry suggest that the Church's ineffectiveness in the past has been due to the fact that she has been preaching an incomplete Gospel. An impressive number are now agreeing with Dr. Bell when he says: "We are at last beginning to understand that healing of the sick is a must in Christian obligation. Jesus said, 'Preach the gospel, heal the sick.' " He meant what He said.

Having observed the magnificent results of the complete Gospel taught, my wonder is not that there should be a resurgence of spiritual healing in the middle of the twentieth century, not that so many churches are reviving that ancient and powerful ministry, but that every church in Christendom has not already incorporated it into its active spiritual life. When that day comes, and it would seem to be on its way, we will become, as Dr. Alfred Price puts it, "walking miracles of God's grace."

The corporate faith of the Church is growing in direct proportion to the vitality of its healing ministry; likewise, as the Church has returned to the historic faith, her spiritual strength has correspondingly increased.

We have never lived by His words, nor dared to claim His promises. Today, led by His Church, and strengthened by the visible truth of His teaching, we are making our first tentative attempts. The implications of this new way of life are there for all to see. "My Omnipotence is limited to the extent of your trust." As it grows clear that our own disbelief is the only limit to the power of God, it seems not impossible that our century, the greatest scientific era the world has ever known, will go down in history as the age of miracles.

A short while ago, I heard a sermon in which the congregation was admonished not to expect visions or to look for great "signs" of God's existence. "Remember," said the priest, "this is the twentieth century. Listen for the still, small voice, and try to recognize it for what it is."

I venture to disagree with this good clergyman.

I think that a merciful God has taken pity on the multitudes who have listened all their lives, in a vain attempt to hear and recognize that "still, small voice."

I believe that the resurgence of Christ's great healing ministry is the evidence the world has so long sought that He still lives. Through spiritual healing comes the voice of God like the roar of thunder. The most deaf among us cannot fail to hear its message. The healing power of the Holy Spirit, as it is being manifested today, comes to us as a great, flaming sign. The most blind among us cannot fail to see its significance.

9

Does God Send Disease?

WHEN I was a youngster, an event occurred which left an indelible impression on my mind, and determined my religious outlook for many years to come. I was taken to see a relative in the final stages of an incurable disease.

I remember the thin body and the tormented eyes. I remember the lugubrious shaking of heads outside her bedroom door, and I remember most of all the comment I heard, repeated again and again. "It is God's will. We mustn't fight against it." Right then and there were sown the first seeds of my own doubt.

I had been taught to love God, but how could I, or anyone else, honestly love a God who willed such suffering? I had been taught that God was my Father, a Father more kind, more compassionate, more just than even my own human father. I felt that I had been duped. If this tortured body I had just seen were an example of His mercy, I wanted none of it.

My doubt was nurtured through the years by my increasing awareness of suffering in the world. I could discern no plan, no reason in it. The innocent, the guilty; the old, the young; the bad, the good. The hand of God struck mercilessly, and apparently with a careless and sadistic abandon.

By the time I reached adulthood, I was in full accord
with John Stuart Mill: "God is either not omnipotent or
not altogether good."

Years ago, someone remarked to me, "God is not responsible for pain. He does not will suffering." This was the sort
of comment which added fuel to the fire of my repudiation
of God, the Father Almighty. If He did not will it, yet
His children suffered, then, obviously, He was not "almighty." If, on the other hand, He *were* omnipotent and
permitted it, He was a cruel and vengeful God, whom I,
for one, could not and would not worship.

The simplest "out" as far as I was concerned was to
reject any idea of a personal God.

But as spiritual healing had led me to really investigate
the Christian faith, so did the miracles of healing give me
my first glimmer of what I now believe to be one of
Christianity's most cogent truths: that God does not
send disease nor does He will the suffering which is rife in
the world. I was to discover that acknowledgment of this
truth did not, after all, impugn His omnipotence.

The problem of pain in relation to a compassionate and
almighty God is a difficult one. Throughout the ages it has
puzzled far abler minds than mine. Small wonder then
that it proved for me, as it has for so many, one of Christianity's greatest hurdles.

For a while I was ready to give up on it and take the easy
way out: assume that God *did* send disease and suffering,
and accept as fact that writhing bodies were God-sent
crucibles to ensure spiritual purification. And then I saw a
good, courageous man in the prime of life, dying by inches,
in agony; an agony which seemed to supersede mind or
spirit; an agony which reduced him to the level of a

wounded jungle animal, for whom pain was the only reality. His eyes glazed with the now ineffective morphine, I heard him gasp a week before he died, "It's lucky I did my praying before. I can't concentrate now on anything except the pain."

Once again my old rebellion flared. Love a God whose love for His children included inflicting upon them the tortures of the damned? I knew that many Christians professed love for such a God. Then they were made of sterner stuff than I.

What, then, was the answer? I turned again to Scripture.

As I reread the Gospels, I wondered briefly if I were completely on the wrong track. Could it be that man's idea of "love" and "good" was wholly different from God's? And then I came to our Lord's own words: "If ye then, being evil, know how to give good gifts unto your children, how much more (of the *same* things, not *different*) shall your Father which is in heaven give good things to them that ask him?" (Matthew 7:11). I had my answer.

I thought again of the healings. Surely God would not perform His healing miracles were it His desire that we remain afflicted. It simply didn't make sense that He would go against His own will by curing the sick.

I saw in Jesus' life a saga of His unremitting labor to assuage and eradicate the pain of men. Would He, who so often proclaimed, "I and my Father are one," work ceaselessly against His Father's will?

Although man may never know the full answer to the *why* of pain, he holds in his knowledge, however incomplete, the most vital essence of a great Christian truth: God does not send or will the disease which cripples so many here on earth.

"I am come that they might have life, and that they might have it more abundantly" (John 10:10).

This theme rings and reverberates throughout the Gospels, and His miracles of physical healing provide ample evidence that He was not referring solely to spiritual life, but the life of the whole man—soul, mind, and body.

Try as I might, I could find no Scriptural evidence whatsoever to support the belief that a pain-racked body provides a more effective receptacle for spiritual grace.

This does not mean that suffering never produces spiritual benefits. Upon occasion it undeniably does. What it does mean, I believe, is that disease and suffering are in no way necessary for spiritual progress. If they were, would Jesus have jeopardized the souls of those who came to Him by alleviating their pain in every instance?

There is no record of Jesus' ever refusing to heal on the grounds that physical well-being would deter spiritual growth. On the contrary, He used the healing power then, as He does now, to bring souls to God. He rebuked sickness as an evil thing, contrary to God's will. "He rebuked the fever; and it left her: and immediately she arose and ministered unto them" (Luke 4:39).

But, you may ask, what about St. Paul's "thorn in the flesh"? If God permitted Paul to suffer physical affliction, how can any of us hope to be healed?

It behooves us to remember that the theory that the "thorn" referred to physical disease is pure conjecture, and was vigorously repudiated by early eminent churchmen, including St. Augustine and St. Chrysostom. Some modern theologians are reverting to the hypothesis that the thorn was, in truth, the sin of spiritual pride, implanted by the devil. In other words, Paul was being persistently tempted and buffeted, as were all the saints, by a "messenger of Satan."

"And lest I should be exalted above measure through the abundance of the revelations," says Paul, "there was given to me a thorn in the flesh, the messenger of Satan to buffet me, lest I should be exalted above measure" (II Cor. 12:7). God's answer to Paul's entreaties "that it might depart from me" was the same assurance of His victorious power which He gives to all of us who, acknowledging our weakness, seek to overcome evil. "My grace is sufficient for thee: for my strength is made perfect in weakness" (II Cor. 12:9).

Those clergymen who reject the theory of Paul's disease remind us that the figure of speech "thorn in the flesh" is used only three times in the Bible. In the first two it obviously refers to enemies of God's purpose, not physical illness. Why, then, they ask, should the meaning of the phrase be distorted in Paul's case to suggest disease?

It is also pointed out that Paul's ministry abounded in miraculous healings. His steadfast confidence in the will of God to heal was an outstanding attribute of his ministry. How, they ask, could he have been so sure, had he himself remained unhealed?

But regardless of learned theological interpretation, the reading of Scripture makes one fact entirely clear: Jesus never told the afflicted that it was good for their souls to suffer, and therefore they had better remain unhealed. No—"There went power out of Him, and healed them all." In view of this alone, it seems hardly reasonable to suppose that He would have made a glaring exception of one of His own Apostles.

"Know ye not that your body is the temple of the Holy

Ghost?" (I Cor. 6:19). Did God will His temple contaminated with disease and corrupted by sin? The answer seems to me self-evident.

If Christ came to redeem mankind, He also came to reveal to men the true nature of God. Again I was forced to revert to the old theme song of "All or Nothing." For if I am to believe in the redemptive mission of Jesus Christ, then I must believe also in His revelation of an all-good, merciful, and loving God. "Be ye therefore merciful as your father is merciful," said Christ. Can we then attribute to God cruelty which the most barbarous among us would hesitate to commit?

Now comes the inevitable question. If God does not will suffering, and yet permits it, how can He be omnipotent?

The answer to this is not simple, any more than Christianity itself is simple. But although "we must trust in the Lord with all our hearts, and lean not unto our own understanding," I believe that the question need not be intellectually circumvented. It can, in my opinion, be met head-on, and at least a partial explanation found.

This lies in the theory of Christian dualism which has always been part of the faith. Christianity acknowledges a state of war between good and evil—a battle between two forces, the one led by God and the other by Satan. This does not imply that there is more than one God. As C. S. Lewis points out, the devil is in reality a parasite, not an independent thing. He was created good by God, and fell from grace. He has perverted his intelligence and will, originally derived from God, to evil use. He can never triumph over God, for to the Creator must go the ultimate victory, but he can hinder and temporarily delay the perfect execution of God's will for us.

The modernist shrugged off the concept of the devil when he shed fundamentalism, but an increasing number of advanced thinkers are returning to the doctrine of Satan as the most logical explanation of suffering and evil in a world created good.

We have smiled superciliously at the Biblical concept of the devil, discarding it as childish fantasy, as we have, from the heights of our spurious intellectual superiority, discarded so many other Christian tenets. We have not realized that we can find in Satan a partial explanation of the God we profess to worship.

Throughout the New Testament, we read of a Dark Power, an evil spirit, who was held to be the power behind sin and its concomitants, disease and death.

"Put on the whole armour of God, that ye may be able to stand against the wiles of the devil. For we wrestle not against flesh and blood, but against principalities, against powers, against the rulers of the darkness of this world" (Eph. 6:11, 12).

To our Lord, Satan was a very real and formidable adversary during His Temptation in the wilderness. The devil "departed from Him for a season," but he was to return and plague Christ's Disciples as he does us. "Simon, Simon, behold, Satan hath desired to have you ... But I have prayed for thee, that thy faith fail not" (Luke 22: 31, 32).

It is interesting to note that those who have been closest to Christ, from His Disciples to the modern saints, have been the most certain of the reality of Satan. The stories of their lives reveal their unremitting battle against the evil spirits.

Now you may not believe in an actual devil, but I think most will agree that there seem to be powers of evil opposing God's perfect will for the world, and deflecting it from its intention. This does not mean that God is not almighty, any more than it means that He is not omnipotent. He chose to create us with free will, which we often misuse, rather than as automatons, guaranteed to carry out His plan for us.

It seems to me that much of our confusion regarding God's omnipotence is due to our human and therefore finite interpretation of the word "almighty." God is almighty in love and power. He conquers slowly by these methods the force which is evil, but He conquers surely. His triumph will ultimately be complete.

His way is a strange blending of the present and the future. Although the Kingdom of God is not entirely beyond this world, neither is it wholly realizable here on earth. Christianity assures us that God will conquer sin and evil, but in His own way and in His own time. His way may be, for us, inscrutable and His time not computable by human standards, but this does not mean that He is withholding from those of us now on earth all knowledge of His Kingdom. In many ways, perhaps most dramatically through His physical healings and spiritual regeneration, He is giving us a foretaste of it, here and now.

There are certain parts of Holy Scripture which may seem contradictory and confusing, but of God's will for us, Jesus leaves us in no doubt.

"He that hath seen me, hath seen the Father" (John 14:9). And He healed bodies and souls wherever He went.

"Go in peace and be whole of thy plague," He said to Lydia.

"Receive thy sight," was His reply to the blind beggar.

"Be thou clean," His answer to the leper. Wherever He went, "As many as touched Him were made whole."

Time and time again, Jesus shows us that disease is contrary to the will of His Father, and therefore, evil.

The late Rev. Richard Spread has stated: "I do not know of any other revelation which Christ gave us, which is so clear as His revelation in regard to this matter. (God's will in regard to disease.) It is indeed so convincing that it seems to me we must either accept it or tear up our New Testament as untrustworthy."

But where, then, in the face of what seems unimpeachable Scriptural evidence, did the pernicious theory originate that God wanted us to suffer, and how did it gain such widespread and long-lasting credence among so many Christians?

As Evelyn Frost points out in *Christian Healing*, when the healing power within the Church began to diminish, the Church was forced to rationalize her failure to heal. As an alibi for her weakened spiritual power, she asserted that God had withdrawn the gift given to His Apostles. She began to teach that God no longer "willed" to heal.

Dr. Leslie D. Weatherhead (*Psychology, Religion, and Healing*) writes: "When in the Gospel narrative we see Christ healing disease, we have evidence that the ideal intention of God is perfect health; and the heresy which attributes illness to personal or family sin is exploded by His touch."

Yet the Church was guilty of this heresy, renouncing Christ's teaching ("Neither hath this man sinned, nor his parents" John 9:3), and declaring that disease was a direct punishment for sin, and, as such, must not be interfered with.

The importance of sin had not been underestimated in the early post-apostolic days of the Church, but the emphasis of unction had been on physical healing. "Is any sick among you? let him call for the elders of the church; and let them pray over him, anointing him with oil in the name of the Lord: And the prayer of faith shall save the sick, and the Lord shall raise him up; and if he have committed sins, they shall be forgiven him" (James 5:14, 15). The "prayer of faith" came first at that time.

When the faith of the Church weakened, and as physical healings, no longer awaited in expectant faith, ceased to occur, the meaning of unction gradually changed until it dealt exclusively with the forgiveness of sin. By 1549, the Council of Trent taught that unction "blots out sins, if any remain to be expiated," thus strengthening the soul of the patient that he might "bear more easily the . . . sufferings of disease . . . and *sometimes* when it is expedient for the soul's salvation, recover bodily health."

The implication in some parts of the Book of Common Prayer that sickness is a "visitation" from God has done much to perpetuate the fallacious doctrine advanced by the weakened Church as an excuse for her failure to heal.*

That God sends disease was a too-glib explanation of a deep-seated problem. As E. Frost comments, it was far easier for the Church to claim that suffering was the cross God meant us to carry, than it was to examine herself to discover wherein lay her own failure of spiritual power.

As a natural sequence to her expedient "explanation," there followed the theory that physical pain was essential for spiritual growth and the soul's salvation. It was never

---

* Studies are now under way for revision of "The Order for the Visitation of the Sick" which will more accurately present the Church's viewpoint on disease.

explained why, if disease were according to God's will, our Lord healed so many. The fact that "great multitudes followed Him, and He healed them all" was simply overlooked.

Jesus "gave them power and authority over all devils, and to cure diseases. And he sent them forth to preach the kingdom of God, and to heal the sick . . . And they departed, and went through the towns, preaching the gospel, and healing everywhere" (Luke 9: 1, 2, 6).

Could the Son of God have mistaken His Father's intent?

If you are sick, and it comforts you in any way to believe that God sent your illness, then, for you, such a belief may be right. For me, it would be wrong, for I could not hold to this belief without sacrificing what I am convinced is Christian truth on the altar of expediency. On the basis of what seems to me to be irrefutable Scriptural evidence, supported by the leaders of spiritual healing and verified by today's healing miracles, I am convinced that disease, like sin, is evil. I believe that as Christians, we should no more resign ourselves to the one than to the other. I believe that in allying ourselves with God, in His fight against evil, He will free us spiritually, and usually physically, from the Dark Powers.

I have not overlooked the fact that many of the saints accepted the theory that God sends suffering as a means of spiritual growth. They saw in their own afflictions a means of increasing their spiritual stature, and they utilized that means to the fullest extent. And in many cases, this is true today. Although pain is often apt to be a demoralizing, sterile thing, forcing concentration on the body to the exclusion of the soul, it is not always wasted. There are many Christians who heroically endure pain with incredible courage, using it to strengthen them spiritually, and bring them closer to God. They are magnificently proving the truth of Christ's saying that in our endurance, we win possession of our souls.

Nevertheless, however ably we may be able to convert the evil of suffering to a holy purpose, the pain itself did not emanate from God. If we can use it to His Glory, we indeed know the triumph of God over the evil spirits. But this does not alter the fact that He did not *create* the evil of suffering. He has simply overcome it.

"There was given to me a thorn in the flesh, *the messenger of Satan* to buffet me . . ." (II Cor. 12:7). There is the argument, and certainly it is not without merit, that suffering develops character. So does the conquest of sin. Fighting on the side of God against evil of any kind develops our spiritual muscles, and brings us closer to Him and to His Kingdom.

Dr. Spread voices the opinion that the mental and moral struggle against sin is a sufficient crucible to ennoble the soul without the addition of physical agony. I must agree with him, for, as far as I can discover, this is what Christ taught.

Our Lord never underestimated the roughness of the road to holiness. He never implied that His way was the easy way. He warned His Disciples of the moral and spiritual temptations to which they would be submitted. He told them to be prepared to suffer persecution for their faith. He never, however, inferred that it was *God* who would be responsible for either their spiritual or physical torments.

Some months ago, I drove a neighbor to her doctor's office, where, for some time, she had been undergoing treatment for a painful disease.

"I guess I shouldn't complain," she sighed. "Sometimes I wonder why God wants me to suffer, but then I realize that it is His will and I shouldn't question it."

As I listened to her comment, I couldn't help but wonder at her inconsistency. If she were so sure that God intended her to suffer, why was she so flagrantly flouting His intention by going to a doctor to alleviate her pain? So it is with all who believe that it is God's will that they suffer. To be consistent, they should believe that all doctors, nurses, and they themselves, as patients, as well as those who pray for their recovery, are deliberately working against the will of God. Do they?

If God's will for us is perfect and abundant health, what about death? Isn't the deterioration of bodily tissues inevitable as part of His creation?

There is a sharp division of opinion on this matter. Some theologians theorize that deterioration of tissue is *not* part of His creation, but came about as a result of man's Fall. They claim that physical death is not at all a "natural" process, but a punishment for sin. "Death ceases in the world when the sin of the world dies."

It is possible that God's original plan for the world, had it been unhampered by sin, might have excluded death of the body. But here we are clearly in the realm of pure conjecture. We simply do not know. What we *do* know, however, is that God does not will mankind to suffer. Man may die, but, as Rebecca Beard says in *Everyman's Search,* he doesn't have to die sick!

Ideally, according to God's plan, man grows older until, completely mature, yet perfect, he falls from the tree of life like a ripened apple, uncontaminated by disease and suffering, unracked by pain.

I believe, on the basis of what I, myself, have seen, that if a man of eighty is *alive*, he should no more live blinded or deaf than a man of thirty. He can be healed, regardless of age.

This, of course, brings up the problem of how to pray in the case of an elderly person suffering intolerable pain. Should we pray for a physical healing, or should we ask that a merciful God take him in death?

There can be no answer to this question except as it comes from God, through prayer, in each individual case. I, who have known a man of seventy-five and a woman of eighty-two brought back through prayer from the ravages of incurable disease, think that I would be inclined to pray for a healing.

"Health is God's primary will for all His children, and disease is not only to be combatted, but to be combatted in God's Name as a way of carrying out His will . . . However disease is brought about, and in whatever way it may be overruled for good, it is, in itself, evil" (Lambeth Report on the Healing Ministry of the Christian Church).

That God wills disease, and that a tortured body is the most effective channel for the Holy Spirit may seem, on the surface, an easy solution to the complex problem of pain. I believe that we are betrayed by its apparent facileness.

Such a theory seems to me an evasion of the truth as Christ taught it—an hallucination which violates some profoundly basic Christian tenets.

It threatens to distort an optimistic, fighting faith, strong and joyous in its "Good News," into a Buddhist philosophy of resignation, despair, and negativism.

It marks a retrogression to the heathen concept of a cruel and capricious God, a far cry indeed from Christ's revelation of a loving Creator, who knows and cares when even one of His sparrows falls to the ground.

It perverts Christianity into something it was never meant to be. Jesus Christ did not establish a religion based on the mortification of the body; He was the incarnation of a great faith, built on the elevation of the spirit. If we fail to understand this, I believe that, as Christians, we face a very real danger. By fastening our eyes too intently on the Cross, we may become blind to the Resurrection.

IO

What Sicknesses Can Be Healed?

I HAVE the complete conviction that there is no such thing as an incurable disease—and that no one need die in pain . . . There is no such thing as an 'easy' or 'difficult' case of healing in Christ's Name."

These are not the words of an irresponsible religious fanatic. They are those of an eminent physician, Dr. Christopher Woodard, who is combining spiritual healing with his practice of medicine and producing spectacular results.

My own findings lead me to concede the validity of his statement: no disease is hopeless—none incurable.

But what about the medical profession? Where does it fit into the picture?

It has a very definite place in today's scheme of things. Until the truth about spiritual healing is universally accepted, until we understand more about spiritual power, medicine, for most people at least, will continue to be depended upon.

If you feel that medical care is indicated in your case, do not hesitate to consult a doctor. Remember that God is not restricted to only one method of healing. He works through men to heal, as He works through them to manifest His Kingdom. Some are healed without doctors; others are healed through Him *by* doctors. In the final sense, *all* of us are healed by God, for He is the origin of all healing.

The honest doctor will admit that his knowledge falls far short of the ultimate mystery of the human body. The surgeon, no matter how skillful, cannot himself *force* a bone to knit. The physician, regardless of his competency, cannot *coerce* a healthy organ to take over the function of its damaged companion.

The atheist ascribes this un-understood healing process to an unknown factor. The Christian ascribes it to God.

It is not a confession of lack of faith to seek medical aid. God gave us our brains to use. But if you want to receive the maximum benefit from your treatment, receive it in conjunction with spiritual healing. Any doctor who is familiar with the results of such co-operation between science and spiritual healing will verify the remarkably increased effectiveness of medicine under these conditions.

Bear in mind always, that when medicine, limited by man's knowledge, fails, or calls a case "hopeless," God, whose healing power knows no limitations, stands ready to take over. He will heal you if you will turn to Him in complete confidence, without fear or mental reservation.

Remember the words of His Son, Jesus Christ, when He said: "And all things whatsoever ye shall ask in prayer, believing, ye shall receive." Poetic words from the Bible which are not meant to apply to you or me in this day and age? Empty words, repeated by well-meaning theologians and hysterically accepted by a few over-zealous wishful thinkers?

No—they are proven truth. *You* do not have to prove their validity; it has been proved for you, times without number. Your only obligation, if you need a healing, is to claim the promise which for thousands has been fulfilled.

His healing hand is already poised, ready to touch you as soon as you ask, in faith.

Spiritual healing is not for saints, not for a selected few, any more than is medicine. It is for you and for everyone, now, today. It is not an ancient myth, a Biblical fantasy. It is a demonstrable truth, as positively established, for example, as the fact that the blood in your body circulates.

Thousands have seen and known and had scientifically verified their spiritual healings. To them, the healing power has been as indisputably proved as has the circulatory system to the medical profession. There is reliable evidence of the healing power of God. Claim this power, which is yours for the asking. Believe that you will receive, and it will be given you.

Knowing of the tendency to write off healings as hysterical cures, I have purposely concentrated on healings which could not be construed, by any stretch of the imagination, as either hysterical or hypnotic. I have emphasized permanent healings of medically diagnosed organic and congenital disease, rather than the curing of functional ailments.

I have omitted more than a passing mention of those cases which involve neuroticism, although, as Dr. Woodard points out, neurotics suffer illnesses as real as any of those suffering physical disabilities and are frequently impossible to cure by medical or psychological means. Nevertheless, because of the ambiguity of psychosomatic illness and therefore of its cure, I have refrained from citing this type of case.

However, in my emphasis on the spectacular healings of medically diagnosed "hopeless" cases, I may have given the erroneous impression that God concerns Himself *only* with desperate illness. This is far from the truth, but that some people harbor this delusion was made apparent to me some six months ago during a conversation with a fellow reporter.

A year previous to this conversation, I had casually mentioned to the man my research in the field of spiritual healing. At that time he made it plain that he thought the project fantastic, and a complete waste of time.

He was stopped in his tracks when, a short time later, he saw with his own eyes the instantaneous healing of his badly crippled mother. His skepticism proceeded to fall from him like a discarded fur coat on a summer day. From then on, his curiosity and interest in the subject were insatiable.

At our meeting a few months ago he happened to remark, "You know, it's strange, with all the medical progress that's been made, they still can't do anything for mankind's most prevalent ailment—the common, garden variety of headache. Just look at me, for instance. I've been to every doctor in town about my headaches. They all assure me it's nothing serious, but not one of them has been able to help me. Well," he concluded ruefully, "I guess I won't die from them—but they certainly make life miserable."

Aware that my friend was receptive to the idea of spiritual healing. I asked him why he didn't try God for a healing. He looked at me with honest amazement. "Why, that's ridiculous," he said. "God may heal *serious* sicknesses, but I can't expect Him to bother with a simple headache!"

That's where he was wrong, as I've found so many others to be. A God who is a Father, who has counted the hairs on each of His children's heads, knows and *cares* if one of His family is in any way indisposed. *Any* indisposition, however slight, is contrary to His will for us. A cancer is not only as easy for Him to cure as a headache, but He is just as interested in healing the one as the other.

With some difficulty I finally prevailed upon my friend to seek spiritual healing. He attended three services—and since the last, five months ago, he who had averaged two crashing headaches a week has had no sign of one.

But if some believe that God can't be "bothered" with minor ailments, there are others who, although they profess to believe in the healing power, attempt to impose man-made limitations upon Him whose power is without limit. They will ask Him, for example, for the healing of a malignancy, but only if it is in an early stage. If any real organic change has taken place, they feel that the case is "too far gone for even God to heal."

The fallacy of this type of reasoning is illustrated by the case of a woman suffering from a medically diagnosed abdominal cancer in an advanced stage. She had lost a great deal of weight, was in constant pain, and her outlook was bad. In an effort to save or at least prolong her life, surgery was decided upon. It was at this time that she first learned of spiritual healing. She was carried into a healing service a week before the operation was to be performed. She claimed that she had received a healing from God, but her family insisted that she undergo the surgery as scheduled.

When her abdomen was opened, the surgeon's fears appeared to be justified. The growth had, as he suspected, metastasized, invaded, and already partially destroyed vital organs. The usual biopsy procedure was followed, and the operating surgeon was flabbergasted to have the lab report come back negative—no sign of malignancy. Yet the unmistakable evidence of cancer lay before him. He repaired the damage as well as human hands could and sent her back to her room. She startled the hospital force by making a quick and uneventful recovery. Today, four years later, she is enjoying perfect health, her "hopelessly" damaged organs are functioning well, and repeated medical examinations reveal no indication of malignancy.

We have seen evidence again and again that there is no limit to the power of God, that no disease is so hopeless as to be incurable, and no ailment so slight as to be unworthy of His healing touch.

What, then, about the question of regrowing severed limbs? I am frequently asked if I have ever seen such a phenomenon. My answer is "No." The closest I have ever come to anything of this sort was the instant creation of eardrums where there were none before.

Dr. Leslie Weatherhead contends that although no prayer is entirely wasted, it would clearly be a waste of time to pray that a man who has lost his leg might regrow another limb. After the many extraordinary things I have witnessed, I am not prepared to take a dogmatic stand on any phase of healing. I am inclined, however, to agree with Dr. Weatherhead, but on basically different grounds.

I do not believe that the regrowth of limbs is *impossible,* particularly as we have the Scriptural record of Christ and the soldier's ear. Nevertheless, I do believe that it is decidedly unlikely that a limb would be regrown, not because the power of God is inadequate, but because to use

His power in this way would be to take from man his means of salvation—faith—based on our free will to believe or reject our Lord.

If our faith were replaced by absolute knowledge, if God were to become wholly explicable in human terms and completely understandable by finite minds, He would be neither God nor all powerful. For faith, not certainty, is the switch, electrified by repentance, which releases the power of God. It is the conduit, cleared by contrition, through which His power flows. Replace this faith by absolute knowledge, and man has lost the instrument by which the power of God is released to him.

Faith is many things. It is the striving, the reaching out to God, the crucible in which we are purified until we can receive His Spirit. It is the road to our salvation, for "he that believeth shall be saved." It is the torment of searching and desire which leads us to Him, until we know at last "the peace that passeth all understanding." It is the very difficulty of its acquisition which makes its rewards so inestimably great.

I have said that, in my opinion, the present-day miracles of healing are the tangible evidence of the living God. They create belief where before there was only the desire to believe. But they create faith, not certainty. *I am* now convinced that they are of God, but those who have neither the time nor the inclination to examine the facts for themselves will continue to chant in disbelief, "Hysteria," "Wrong diagnosis," "Religious fanaticism."

Others, who have witnessed miracles of healing and in honesty admit their existence, will prate of therapeutic energies released by an unknown scientific law. Thus, the present manifestations of spiritual power leave the way

wide open. Faith is still the key which unlocks the door
of our hearts to God.

To see a severed limb instantly, miraculously restored
destroys faith by pushing it into the realm of complete
certainty. At this exact moment, the vital element of our
salvation must be irrevocably lost.

I do not believe that God will take from us His marvellous gift of free will, to believe or not as we see fit.

I do not believe that He will coerce us into a knowl-
edge-based belief, thereby lifting us out of the sphere of
true faith, upon which rests our means of grace and hope
of salvation.

I do not believe that His power to restore a severed
limb is insufficient. I believe, rather, that His mercy is too
great.

A study of the healing ministry of the Early Church
makes today's miracles less startling and more easily acceptable, although surely no less exciting, than when
approached "cold."

I know from personal experience how long a step it is
from skepticism to a faith which can accept today's
manifestations of the Holy Spirit.

The step is shortened by the realization that the early
Church Fathers were reliable and accurate historians, for
the miracles of healing they painstakingly recounted are
being duplicated today. It may well prove, as Tertullian
contended, that "the flesh acts in the capacity of servant
to the soul." And that as the soul is expunged of guilt
and subsequently healed, the healing of the lesser agent,
the body, will inevitably follow.

The Dark Age of the Church which has lasted sixteen
hundred years is at last near its end. A light now gleams,

puncturing the blackness of the Church's long night. His Spirit is again illuminating His Body for all to see. A compassionate God has raised the curtain on many centuries of darkness. He has taken our hand and is leading us out of the obscurity of our self-imposed bondage of heresy into the clear light of truth—that from Him comes only good.

Today's active healing ministry demonstrates that by positive and affirmative prayer, which creates the same sense of expectancy as was present in the Early Church, any and every ailment, regardless of its nature, responds or can respond to the curative power of the Holy Spirit.

Believing this, "Then the eyes of the blind shall be opened, and the ears of the deaf shall be unstopped. Then shall the lame man leap as an hart, and the tongue of the dumb sing" (Isaiah 35:5, 6).

Today's healing miracles are the direct evidence of God's power; the actual witness of His Son's inestimable love; the visible manifestation of the Holy Spirit.

II

Your Prayer of Faith

THE POWER of Jesus Christ is yours for the asking.
His call "Come unto Me" is not restricted to Methodists or Episcopalians, Roman Catholics or Baptists, Presbyterians or Lutherans. It is for all men, everywhere. He asks only that you go to Him in faith and with the courage to claim His promise that all who ask in His Name shall receive.

For centuries most Christians, as well as non-Christians, have failed to believe the full Gospel because it seemed too good to be true. Today we know that it *is* true. Those who have witnessed the power of the Gospel believe; those who have actually seen the fulfilment of our Lord's stupendous promises no longer doubt that "if you believe, all things are possible."

The first step towards your own healing occurs when you are prepared to accept as truth our Lord's revelation of the nature of God. But your mind's conviction that a merciful God wills for you perfect health is one thing; your heart's knowledge that He will heal you and yours is another. The search for Him can be instigated by the intellect, but He can only be found through faith.

We are told that "the prayer of faith shall save the sick" (James 5:15). But what is that prayer, you ask;

and how can you acquire the faith which will lead you to Him and to His healing power?

There is no use pretending that a simple, unquestioning, child-like faith is easy. For most of us who are the products of a sophisticated, humanistic society, it is prodigiously difficult to lay aside our pseudo-intellectualism of which we are so proud, and believe the words of Jesus Christ simply because He said them. Yet that is what is demanded of us. "Whosoever shall not receive the kingdom of God as a little child, he shall not enter therein" (Mark 10:15). Nowhere do these words apply more forcibly than in the realm of spiritual healing.

In your quest for faith, turn again to the New Testament, this time considering carefully some of the many promises He made you.

"Whatsoever ye shall ask the Father in my name, he will give it you" (John 16:23).

"What things soever ye desire, when ye pray, believe that ye receive them, and ye shall have them" (Mark 11:24).

"And I say unto you, Ask, and it shall be given you; seek, and ye shall find; knock, and it shall be opened unto you" (Luke 11:9). Claim these promises with your mind, today. Tomorrow, you will claim them with your heart. These are the words of the Son of God. Can you, in consistency, accept Christ and His teaching and, at the same time, casually dismiss His solemn pledge as the idle words of an irresponsible deceiver?

If a friend makes you a promise, you don't doubt him. You are not hesitant to predicate your actions on the assumption that he will keep his word. Is the word of Christ then less reliable than that of a friend? Not measuring your faith, but believing what He has told you, "If ye have faith as a grain of mustard seed . . . nothing shall be impossible to you," dare to claim the promises of your God.

But, you object, how can we reconcile the complete assurance of Christ's promises with the words we have been taught are indispensable when addressing our Father: "If it be Thy will"?

Again we find the answer in the Gospels. They leave us in no doubt as to the will of God in regard to healing. There are many occasions in our daily lives when we are not certain of His will. At these times we must seek to learn it, so that we may carry it out. But in the area of sin and disease, His will has been clearly revealed by Jesus. We know through Him that God wills our freedom from sin. He does not will that we murder or steal. He wills our health and abundant life. He does not will sick bodies or diseased souls.

Did Christ say, "Arise and walk, *if it be God's will*"? No. He spoke the words of active faith, the healing prayer of positive affirmation, of resolute command. "Receive thy sight," He said, with certain knowledge that it was the will of God that the blind see.

Following his example, then, we pray for healing, not with the resigned, faith-shattering plea, "If it be Thy will," but with the faith-evoking confidence of complete assurance: "In the Name of Christ I know that I am healed, that *His perfect will may be fulfilled.*"

It is a fundamental psychological maxim that if people go through the proper motions, they soon begin to feel the corresponding emotions. So it is with faith. Go through the motions, exercise that faith which you have, and your heart will react to receive Him.

Attend healing services regularly. The Church has become once more a vast reservoir of Pentecostal power, proving again and again that "things which are impossible with men are possible with God." Draw on this power. Let the healing Church guide you, and the strength of corporate faith sustain and multiply your own.

Seek out those who have felt His touch, for the lamp of faith is lit, taper by taper, one from the other. Let them inspire and teach you. They have traveled the path before you and won their fight for faith.

Christ is with us at all times, but at His Altar you will feel His Presence intensified. Hold up to Him your cup of faith. He will fill it according to your ability to receive.

Your desire for faith is your assurance that you will find it. "Ye shall seek me, and find me, when ye shall search for me with all your heart" (Jeremiah 29:13). But you must seek Him for His own sake. Sometimes in our eagerness to find faith we become confused. We pin our gaze so firmly on faith that we fail to see Him. Tense and anxious, we think we're striving to reach God, when in our hearts we're only seeking to realize His gifts. And this leads us to one of the great paradoxes of spiritual healing. Your willingness *not* to be healed, if only you can know God, often affords you the best assurance of healing. A desire to find God which supersedes the desire for His rewards, the conviction that your soul's salvation is more important than your body's healing, frequently prove the key to total health, for "Whosoever shall seek to save his life shall lose it; and whosoever shall lose his life shall preserve it" (Luke 17:33).

Prayer is our means of communion with God. Through prayer we learn to know and love and trust Him.

We pray with the knowledge that God loves us always, whether or not we love Him. But we know that when we love Him in return, things begin to happen. Through that mutual love pulses His greatest power: the mercy which forgives our sins, and the compassion which heals our bodies. "If a man love me . . . the Father and I will make our abode with him."

We pray with a repentant spirit, asking forgiveness for our sins however inconsequential they may seem: the hasty word spoken at breakfast, the resentment harbored for a wrong done us, the envy we feel for a neighbor's new car. We pray, above all, for forgiveness of that subtle but grave sin, our feeling of separation from God. "If we confess our sins, he is faithful and just to forgive us our sins, and to cleanse us from all unrighteousness" (I John 1:9).

With the first stirrings of recognizable faith, and with infinite hope, we pray with confidence in the authority of His Word, believing His promise that "If ye shall ask anything in my Name, I will do it" (1 John 14:14). Seeing ourselves well and strong, filled with His Life, we pray with the conviction that we shall be healed.

We thank Him for the healing received, knowing that it is already done—for "As thou hast believed, so be it done unto thee" (Matt. 8:13).

We praise Him for the victory, even before it is realized, believing "that it shall be even as it was told me" (Acts 27:25).

We have prayed the prayer of faith. And if our prayer ends with the cry which has echoed down the centuries,

"Lord, I believe; help thou mine unbelief" (Mark 9:24), Jesus will understand. He lived among men, He knows the difficulty of faith, and He will honor our seeking of Him and His truth. He will not fail us, as He did not fail the man who, nearly two thousand years ago, first uttered that cry.

As we struggle to touch the hem of His garment, thrust back from time to time by our own unbelief, we suddenly see in the distance His hands outstretched to us. We surge forward now, in perfect faith. We feel His touch, and hear at last the words: "Go then; thy faith hath made thee whole."

12

Why Some Are Healed and Others Not

WHY are some healed and others not? This question has puzzled many, including myself.

For a long time the healing power appeared to me to be operating at random, touching some and passing by others ostensibly equally worthy or unworthy, however you cared to look at it. It was only after months of investigation and interviewing that I began to discern some order emerging out of what had formerly seemed chaos.

There are, of course, certain cases of failure to heal which seem easily explained in view of what we know about spiritual healing.

Take, for example, the case of a woman who had suffered an incapacitating back injury which failed to respond to medical treatment. Having heard rumors of "miraculous" healings, she decided to try her luck.

"I'm ready to try anything once," she remarked. "If there's any magic floating around I might as well get my share of it!"

Needless to say, she was not healed. (However, impressed, in spite of herself, with what she saw, she is today a member of the Church and feels certain that as her understanding and faith increase, she will receive a healing.)

The idea that there is any "hocus-pocus" involved in spiritual healing is manifestly absurd. To think that there is a "magic" element in the anointing oil, or a "magic" power in the priest's fingers, is a childish and pagan superstition, totally foreign and wholly unacceptable to Christianity.

When spiritual healing, which is essentially spiritual, is approached as though it were some sort of voodoo rite, it is not difficult to understand why Christian healing does not occur. Far more difficult to comprehend, at least at first glance, are those cases of *successful* healings which apparently occur in direct contradiction to the essential principles of spiritual healing as we know them.

Faith and repentance are two basic requisites for healing. Yet what about those who by their own admission lack both, and still experienced dramatic healings? How can this apparent violation of the healing law be justified? In my opinion, based on a detailed study of these cases and the subsequent results of their healings, in two ways.

First, faith, even though not personally held, is still the instigating factor in any individual's healing. Anyone who goes to a healing service attended by other believers is surrounded by an almost palpable aura of faith—an invincible conviction that the power of God is present there, in abundance, to be received. A strong, corporate faith can move mountains. It can also heal and convert an unbeliever.

And here we come to our second point. The primary purpose of all healing is conversion. The history of the Early Church is filled with reliable records of Roman conversions brought about by Christian healing. "And how many men of rank (to say nothing of the common people) have been delivered from devils and healed of diseases. Even Sverus (the Emperor) himself . . . sought out the Christian Proculus . . . in gratitude for his once having cured him by anointing . . ." (Tertullian).

Likewise, the present revival of the healing ministry is proving itself the greatest instrument of conversion to be placed in the hands of the Church since the early post-apostolic days.

Those who are healed through their own faith know God as they never did before. The witness of their healed bodies and reformed lives serves to rekindle the faith of all those who come in contact with them. There are, nevertheless, certain spheres in which the total unbeliever, converted through healing, can operate as a uniquely powerful protagonist for Christianity. His influence extends among those agnostics who might well never be reached in any other way.

Take, for example, a professed agnostic of my acquaintance. He had been the victim, long previously, of an accident which had permanently crippled his right arm. For ten years it had hung useless by his side.

As he walked down the street one morning last spring, he met a friend, an eminent attorney. When they came to the local church, the lawyer said, "I'm going to the weekly healing service in here."

"What on earth is that?" queried my friend.

"I haven't time to tell you now," came the reply. "Why don't you come in and see for yourself?"

"Why I did it, I'm still not sure," relates the former agnostic, "but the first thing I knew, I found myself walking down the church aisle. I sat alone, toward the back of the church, tongue in cheek, and wondered how anyone as intelligent as Jim could be so gullible. As the minister put his hands on Jim's head up there at the Altar, I suddenly felt a wave of heat and something like an electric shock run through my right shoulder. There was a second of excruciating pain, and it was over.

"By the time Jim joined me in my pew after the service, I had begun to think I had imagined the whole thing. Rather shamefaced I told him what had happened. He stared hard at my face. 'Raise your right arm,' he said. I hesitated, and he remarked, apparently without surprise, 'Don't be afraid. You've been healed.' I lifted my arm far above my head. As if in a dream I rose to my feet."

Since then, this man has joined the Church and has told his story far and wide.

Why was this agnostic, faithless and unrepentant, healed? The answer seems self-evident. Not only was *he* brought to God through his healing, but his witness has converted numerous agnostics. The healing of a former unbeliever's body was to awaken their interest as no mere sermon had ever been able to do. The testimony of their erstwhile fellow-agnostic was to convince them, as nothing else could, of the existence of a living God. In this man's story we see also how the healing testimony works for God.

The majority of ministers of healing believe that such testimony is a valuable means of evoking faith in others. An outstanding exception to this belief is Dr. Weatherhead. He bases his opposition on the words of Jesus, who said, in effect, "Go and tell no man."

The reason for Christ's adjuration to silence is unknown. However, as it occurred early in His ministry, it seems reasonable to assume that He knew the circumstances to be unpropitious because of the total unpreparedness of the people. Later in His ministry, we see many more recorded instances when Jesus commanded those healed to relate their news far and wide. "Go home to thy friends, and tell them how great things the Lord hath done for thee . . ." (Mark 5:19), seems to be the rule, not the exception.

In view of the Gospel records and my own observation, I can only believe that testimonies are vitally important and invaluable contributions to the cause of Christ. My conviction that the divine purpose behind the revealed healing ministry is conversion, and that miraculous healing is proving itself today, as it has in the past, one of Christianity's most potent weapons towards that end, is not idle conjecture.

By the witness of those healed, I have seen a dim faith galvanized into dynamic action, a pale belief vivified into a flaming sword.

For every witness to His healing touch, scores more are healed because of their new knowledge that He lives. For every witness to His compassion, hundreds fall to their knees in unaccustomed prayer.

Seeing and hearing the tangible evidence of His good works, new multitudes go on their way glorifying God, saying with their hearts as well as with their lips, "Thine, O Lord, is the greatness, and the power, and the glory, and the victory, and the majesty."

In the beginning of my study of spiritual healing, I was frankly baffled by a number of cases where faith appeared to be present, but healing failed to occur. Close questioning of these cases, however, was to shed considerable light on the mystery.

All those I interviewed believed unequivocally in God

and in His power to heal. What they could not unreservedly believe was that it was His *will* to heal them. A lifetime of teaching that suffering was the will of God could not easily or quickly be eradicated. Spiritual healing for this group was a new and exciting revelation. Like myself a short while back, these individuals accepted intellectually the fact that healings were taking place. They had seen the evidence with their own eyes. But emotionally they were as yet unable to accept the fact that they, too, could receive the healing power.

They claimed faith—and faith in God they most assuredly possessed—but they were confusing their overwhelming desire to be healed with faith in God's will to heal them—of which they were far from sure.

A number of this group admitted that they felt they were not "good" enough to be healed by God—that they thought that only those whom He especially favored could receive His power.

This, of course, is a total misconception of spiritual healing. God does not weigh our merits, but pardons our offenses. All He asks is a contrite heart, a desire to know Him better and to love Him more. There is no instance of Jesus ever having refused to heal anyone because he was a sinner, and there must have been many among the multitudes who came to Him, but "He healed them all." Indeed, our Lord seems to have considered healing a most efficacious way of dealing with sinners.

It is important to remember that it is not sin, but lack of repentance which keeps us from God and constitutes the insuperable barrier against His healing power.

The close connection between repentance and healing

is clearly illustrated in our Lord's healing of the palsied man.

". . . Thy sins are forgiven thee," said Jesus. "Arise, and take up thy couch, and go into thine house. And immediately he rose up before them . . . and departed to his own house, glorifying God" (Luke 5:20, 24-25).

Repentance is perhaps more readily understood by a blackened criminal, who has a specific "crime" for which he can repent, than it is for many of us who, according to society and ourselves, lead blameless lives.

Take, for example, a friend of mine who had been unsuccessfully seeking a healing for months. I was puzzled by his failure, for I knew the man's conviction that Jesus Christ can heal all sickness.

And then one day my friend unwittingly offered the explanation in his words: "I've quit going to church. I'm tired of being told to repent. I give my share to charity. I try not to hurt others. I simply can't see that I have anything to be sorry *for*."

I knew what he meant. I, too, had rebelled against the idea of what I thought was "grovelling" before God in abject humility when I had committed no overt act of wickedness. This too-common unawareness of the reality of spiritual sin, which leads to a misapprehension of the act of repentance, has locked many hearts against God, blocking the channel through which His healing power must flow.

But remember, if *under*-emphasizing our sin is detrimental, so is *over*-emphasizing it. There are those so filled with self-reproach, so falsely convinced of their own unworthiness, that they cannot accept the fullness of God's forgiveness.

In the types of cases I have so far mentioned, the reasons for lack of healing seem fairly obvious. There remains, however, one other group in which healing of the body occasionally fails to result. I refer to those whose faith in the healing power of Christ and whose understanding of the act of contrition cannot reasonably be questioned.

The Gospels tell us, "All who touched Him were made perfectly whole."

Irenaeus claimed, "No one who believes on Christ shall remain unhealed."

Yet I know a man who is conducting a remarkable healing ministry who has himself not been healed of a minor affliction which has plagued him for years. While it is true that only God can gauge the degree of faith in a human heart, we can assume in this instance that the minister in question has faith. While it is true that only God can know the sincerity of our repentance, we can assume that this man knows true contrition. Why, then, should he who possesses the keys to the Kingdom in the form of true faith and honest repentance be denied the fruits of that Kingdom here on earth, which many less worthy are enjoying?

The answer, I believe, still hinges largely on faith: it is not, in this case, attributable to the lack of faith of one individual, but to the faithlessness of the Church as a whole.

Jesus, during His earthly ministry, was unable to heal in an atmosphere of disbelief. There were towns of which it was said that "he did not many mighty works there because of their unbelief" (Matthew 13:58).

This would seem to be our assurance, then, that when failures occur among the faithful, it is not the will of God but human weakness which is responsible.

Already the results of the rapidly increasing corporate faith of the Church are evidenced in the steady decline in number of failures to heal. Dr. Robert Bell estimates that in the past few years these failures have decreased by over 40%.

In the Early Church, the onus of faith was never placed entirely on the individual alone. Friends, relatives, and the whole Church prayed for the patient's recovery. If healing failed to occur, the Church considered such failure a sin on her part, not on the part of the patient.

While today's resurgence of the healing ministry has resulted in a growing public acceptance of spiritual healing, such acceptance is obviously far from universal. There are many churches where successful healing ministries are being conducted, yet a large segment of the congregation does not believe in it. This can well create that atmosphere of unbelief which makes it difficult for Christ to work.

But if the faithful can remain physically unhealed because of the faithlessness of the Church, how can any of us hold that unreserved faith which is a vital requirement of effective spiritual healing? Don't these failures create in our minds an element of doubt? They need not.

You will note that in every reference to failure as applied to the faithful, I have spoken of "physical" healing, for, according to all available records, the souls of the faithful are inevitably healed to a degree which no one who has not undergone the experience can possibly comprehend.

I have said that the primary purpose of healing is to bring the individual to God, because I have observed how infinitely more wonderful than the curing of a sick body is the healing of the soul, which is part of all spiritual healing. No one who has ever felt the healing touch will deny that this is true, and in those cases where believers remain physically unhealed, this is true to an extraordinary degree. Those whose healing has been limited to the soul seem to experience an exceptionally powerful regeneration which enables them to triumph completely over their physical handicaps, using them for the advance of His Kingdom.

The case of a woman acquaintance is typical of this category. A person of unlimited faith in the healing power of Christ, she sought, and has thus far failed, to receive a physical healing. Her family was extremely apprehensive that her experience would cause her to lose her faith in God. To the contrary, she received a degree of grace and underwent a spiritual regeneration which soon became dramatically apparent to all who knew her. She became a bulwark of spiritual strength and has been personally responsible for the institution of healing services in some eleven churches.

If you have faith, yet so far have not received a physical healing, do not feel that it is necessarily your own lack which is impeding your recovery. While it would be impossible to overestimate the importance and value of personal faith, bear in mind the possibility that the weakened faith of the whole Church may be hindering Christ's power. If this is so, you are far from helpless, for here is where intercessory prayer enters the picture.

His words of promise, that when two or three are gathered together in His Name, He will grant their requests, have never been proved so valid as in the field of spiritual healing.

You want to be healed, and God longs to heal you, but perhaps the healing is conditional on corporate and co-operative faith and prayer. Remember that the paralyzed man at Capernaum might never have been healed had not his four friends, strong in their faith, brought him to the feet of Jesus. "Jesus seeing their faith" healed him.

Just as the Early Church recognized the importance of corporate prayer in healing, so do the most successful of the healing ministries today.

The power of corporate prayer is illimitable. So vital to the healing ministry does the Rev. Richard Spread consider prayer groups organized for the specific purpose of praying for the sick, that he urges that the *first* step for any minister interested in administering spiritual healing should be to form such a prayer circle in his parish.

Dr. Christopher Woodard knows well the power of corporate prayer, so dramatically illustrated in the miraculous healing of his own son.

The child, desperately ill with cerebro-spinal meningitis, had been given up by the hospital physicians. Dr. Woodard points out: "Being myself a Harley Street physician, I had the most eminent medical men at my beck and call. When I saw my son's condition, I did not 'beck' or 'call' any of them. I immediately rang up an Anglican priest, himself a healer, in Suffolk—and asked him to pray as he had never prayed before."

The doctor also notified a number of other churches, so that his son was prayed for by many hundreds of people.

At one time during this period, Dr. Woodard walked into his son's hospital room and found the boy's face covered with a towel. The hospital thought him dead.

The child made a miraculous recovery, as his father had known he would, to the stupefaction of the hospital staff.

"According to your faith be it unto you"—but upon occasion the faith of one individual, however strong, is not quite strong enough to raise the iron curtain of unbelief which has for so many centuries shrouded the truth for so many people. But as corporate faithlessness can sometimes hinder the healing power of the living Christ, so, again and again, has the power of corporate faith proved itself to be without limit or boundary.

Obviously, none of us can fully comprehend God's entire purpose in healing, but that it is His will to heal cannot, in my opinion, be reasonably disputed.

After a prolonged study of spiritual healing, I am unalterably convinced that no one need remain unhealed if he fully realizes and wholly accepts the power and will of God to heal; if he purifies himself through the Sacraments; if he draws inspiration from the faith of others; and if he asks for and receives intercessory prayer.

A church prelate said to me not long ago, "You know, if an evangelist said to me, 'Brother, are you saved?' I'd be in the embarrassing position of having to say, 'No!' The truth is, I hope I'm in the *process* of being saved here on earth—but I certainly can't say I'm saved until I reach Heaven."

I think it is important that we realize this same truth about healing. Today's healing miracles are indeed a foretaste of the Resurrection, but just as we cannot know full salvation except in Heaven, so we cannot know, until then, complete healing of the body, soul, and spirit.

13

Methods of Healing Within the Church

THERE are many churches doing a remarkable healing work which make little or no use of the sacramental rites. This would seem to indicate that the great principles which underlie the sacramental methods can be adapted or utilized to meet the needs of every church.

It is abundantly clear that the Church's ministry of healing is not confined to any one denomination. It belongs to every branch of the Church Universal. "The heaven and heaven of heavens cannot contain thee; how much less this house that I have builded?" (I Kings 8:27).

However, as we find a sacramental Church, the Episcopal, well in the vanguard of spiritual healing; as we note the number of non-liturgical churches with outstanding healing ministries which now administer one or more of the sacramental healing rites, it would appear that His recreating life is made more easily available through the Sacraments.

A clergyman at an interdenominational meeting held in March, 1954, attempting to analyze the success of the Episcopal Church's healing ministry, commented: ". . . I think it points out that the Sacraments or the outward signs of something, whether it be by word, touch or any of the various symbols, have tremendous healing power."

This is perhaps not surprising, as we realize that behind the Sacraments lies the historical precedent established by our Lord and the Apostles. They are the historically verified means of opening the channel through which the healing power of God may flow unimpeded. While it is true that we cannot know God through the Sacraments alone, through them we may more readily touch His hand. As the outward and visible signs of His grace and love, they inspire the confidence and arouse the expectant faith so many of us lack. For those too sick to concentrate on prayer, the concrete, physical signs of God's grace provide incalculable comfort.

As 65% of all healing within the organized Church takes place in the Episcopal, it has proved of considerable interest to me to examine the methods used in this Church.

There appear to be certain basic factors which are always essential to spiritual healing anywhere: repentance, faith, thanksgiving, and praise—all expressed acts of the pervading love which is the bedrock foundation of all spiritual experience. To these factors, the Episcopal Church adds emphasis on the Sacraments, but, at the same time, does not subtract the freedom which permits laymen with outstanding healing gifts to work within the framework of the Church. Increasingly aware that these elements of freedom plus sacramental emphasis were characteristic of the Early Church where healing flourished, clergymen and laymen alike are today regarding the Sacraments with new interest.

"I cannot help but believe," says a minister who has studied spiritual healing in all branches of the Church, "that in the general over-all Protestant tradition, we back away too much from the sacramental paraphernalia. I think this is indicated by the fact that when an Episcopal church opens its doors offering these healing services, a preponderant number of people who take advantage of them are not those to whom the Sacraments are an everyday affair, but people who have perhaps not been brought up in that tradition at all."

What are those specific healing rites, sacramental in nature, to which the Episcopal Church so strictly adheres in her healing ministry? They are those commonly used in the Early Church: the laying-on-of-hands, Holy Unction, and the ministry of Confession and Absolution.

The Church derives her authority for the laying-on-of-hands from the Gospels, which record our Lord's frequent use of this rite for healing purposes: "He laid his hands on every one of them, and healed them" (Luke 4:40). "Jesus put forth his hand and touched him" (Matt. 8:3). "Come and lay thy hand upon her and she shall live" (Matt. 9:18).

As His touch appeared then to be the channel for divine grace, so for nearly two thousand years has the laying-on-of-hands been closely associated with the operation of the Holy Spirit, used by the clergy as an outward sign of spiritual grace.

Since the revival of spiritual healing, the meaning of the laying-on-of-hands has been extended to include, as it did in the Early Church, healing of the body. The use of this Sacrament, as well as that of Holy Unction, is by no means confined to the Episcopal Church. Dr. Albert Day, for example, pastor of a large Methodist church in Baltimore, where he is conducting one of the great healing ministries of the Church, lays hands on all who attend the healing services, as well as anointing any who desire unction. The Rev. William Holmes, an outstanding Presbyterian healer, says: "I believe in the laying-on-of-hands. I accept it as a warranted and authentic technique." A number of Presbyterian clergy regularly anoint. Only recently I noted a remarkable cancer healing which immediately followed administration of the rite.

As a symbol of God's healing intention, the imposition of hands appears to be a valuable psychological aid to the sick, but its effects, curiously enough, are far more than purely psychological. The hands of the officiant seem to serve as actual transmitters of the healing power. Time after time, even the most prosaic of those who received the Sacrament report: "When hands were laid on, I felt a sensation of terrific heat course through my body," or "I felt a sensation like an electric shock."

It is this sort of phenomenon, as well as the healings themselves, which has intrigued the curiosity of numerous scientists who are doing investigative work on the subject to the gratification of everyone who has a sincere interest in spiritual healing. As Dr. Otis Rice, Executive Director of the National Council of Churches of Christ, comments: "We are most interested in furthering spiritual healing. We welcome scientific research, for we want to keep our feet very much on the ground."

Holy Unction is the formal Church Sacrament which for centuries has existed primarily for the healing of the sick in body and mind.

The Disciples were sent forth by Jesus anointed with oil. "They anointed with oil many that were sick, and healed them" (Mark 6:13).

A great many clergymen today use Holy Unction interchangeably with the laying-on-of-hands, but some feel that its use must be guarded. There is still the possibility of adverse psychological effect on some individuals, who subconsciously associate anointing with extreme unction. The perversion of the *healing* Sacrament of the Early Church into a ritual for impending death has created an impression which is slow to be entirely eradicated.

As Holy Unction is the Sacrament expressly intended for healing of the body and mind, the Sacrament of Penance exists specifically for the healing of the soul and spirit. In the final sense, of course, the two are inextricably woven together and interdependent. Sin is a spiritual disorder as disease is a physical one. The healing of the whole man is clearly dependent on curing both soul and body.

The subject of sin and the necessity for repentance is unpopular. It took me a long time to realize, and a longer time to admit, that whether we like it or not, repentance and absolution is the core of the Church's ministry today as it has been for hundreds of years. It is also the heart of the healing ministry.

Our Lord said that "Repentance and remission of sins should be preached in his name among all nations" (Luke 24:47). Every branch of the Church provides some means of Confession, whether it be obligatory private Confession as in the Roman Catholic Church, or the corporate general Confession which is provided by every Protestant denomination within the framework of its own particular service. The Episcopal ministry of Confession and Absolution includes not only the corporate Confession, but private sacramental Confession for any individual who may desire it. "If there be any of you, who . . . cannot quiet his own conscience . . . let him come to me, or to some other Minister of God's Word, and open his grief . . ." (Book of Common Prayer, p. 88).

The idea of private Confession is distasteful to many Protestants, but interestingly enough, it seems to be growing increasingly palatable. Psychologists have discovered the therapeutic value of unburdening one's guilt, which the Church has known for centuries. The assurance of absolution has a purifying and revivifying spiritual effect which is difficult to attain in any other manner. I remember one woman telling me with a smile: "The first time I made my confession I was acutely conscious of the disapproval of my stern Presbyterian forebears, but when the Absolution was pronounced, I was flooded with a sense of such peace and joy that I have returned at regular intervals ever since. The Sacrament quickens my conscience, and I feel that it is helping me to grow in grace."

You may object that only God can forgive sin—that no man has that power. You are entirely correct. The Episcopal Church claims the authority to grant Absolution, not in its own name, but in the Name of Christ. ". . . as my Father hath sent me, even so send I you . . . Receive ye the Holy Ghost: Whose soever sins ye remit, they are remitted unto them; and whose soever sins ye retain, they are retained" (John 20: 21-23).

The Church continues, through her ministry of Confession and Absolution, to carry out this Apostolic commission. God forgives; the words of the priest simply convey that forgiveness. The Sacrament of Penance is again the symbol, the outward sign, which brings closer the reality of the living God, affording ineffable comfort to many contrite hearts. There is in this Sacrament no implication of intercession, no question of a mediator pleading our cause to an inaccessible God. It is merely a sacramental method of Confession which helps to clear the channel for the inflow of God's purifying power.

Perhaps the Confessional's greatest practical value lies in its demand for thorough self-examination: the necessity of carefully enumerating our faults. In private prayer there is a tendency to deprecate and to alibi our shortcomings. While one part of the mind prays, "Forgive me, Lord, for harboring resentment," the other part is busy justifying: "After all, he *did* play a dirty trick on me. How can I *not* resent it?"

The nature of the corporate Confession, as it is a general statement of our sinfulness rather than an explicit accounting of our faults, tends to make us gloss over any specific wrongdoings of which we may be guilty. The end of our general Confession is likely to leave us as uncertain of God's forgiveness as we are indefinite about our sins. It is the explicit *defining* of our faults which gives them substance—a substance which they *must* assume if we are to know the reality of Absolution.

But the love and mercy of God are obviously not restricted to those who partake of a sacramental rite. St. John assures us that "If we confess our sins, he is faithful and just to forgive us our sins, and to cleanse us from all unrighteousness" (I John 1:9). The only thing that really matters is that we ask, with sincerity and humility, the forgiveness of Jesus, secure in the knowledge that He will absolve us, "making clean our hearts within us."

This might be a good place to interject a word on the spiritual value of fasting—not as a penance, but as a means of quickening the spirit, authorized by Christ, and used extensively in the healing ministry of the Early

Church. "When ye fast, be not, as the hypocrites, of a sad countenance . . . But thou, when thou fastest, anoint thine head, and wash thy face; That thou appear not unto men to fast, but unto thy Father which is in secret: and thy Father, which seeth in secret, shall reward thee openly" (Matt. 6:16-18).

So many cases have come to my attention where fasting has immediately preceded miraculous healing, that there can be no doubt that the denial of the body makes us singularly receptive to the Holy Spirit. Long aware of this truth, the Episcopal Church urges that communicants fast before partaking of the Lord's Supper.

And this brings us to the subject of Holy Communion— one of the two great Sacraments ordained by Christ.

Although not specifically a "healing" Sacrament, there is mounting evidence that it is perhaps the greatest of all healing services. The clergy tends to echo the words of Gladys Falshaw, noted Anglican healer: "We still don't fully realize what we have in Holy Communion. We are just beginning to scratch the surface of the unlimited healing power inherent in this Sacrament."

St. Paul was well aware of the tremendous healing virtue in this great Christian act of worship (I Cor. 11:26-29), and we are told that the early Christians "ate it with wild joy," knowing that it was the source of their physical and spiritual strength.

As a layman, I have been immeasurably impressed with the healing results which so often follow the administration of Holy Communion today. I have neither the temerity nor the knowledge to attempt an explanation of why these remarkable manifestations of the healing power so often occur following the Lord's Supper. However, tak-

ing into account the small knowledge of spiritual healing
we now possess, there would seem to be certain factors in
the Communion Service which might offer at least a
partial explanation of its healing propensities.

God is always accessible to us wherever we may be, and
the working of the Holy Spirit is certainly not confined to
the Altar rail. However, as our Lord is present in an inexplicable way during the Sacrament which He ordained,
so, within the service of Holy Communion appear to be
concentrated all those elements necessary to spiritual healing—sanctified and illuminated by the Holy Spirit.

In the light of increased understanding, the invitation
to Holy Communion assumes a new and deeper significance.

"Ye who do truly and earnestly *repent* you of your
sins, and are in *love* and *charity* with your neighbours . . .
Draw near with *faith*, and . . . make your humble *confession* to Almighty God . . ." We are now more fully
aware of the implication in these words; we comprehnd
more completely the obligation as well as the opportunity
involved in our response.

"The Body of our Lord Jesus Christ, which was given
for thee, preserve thy *body* and soul unto everlasting
life." We recognize here a statement of deliverance for
the *whole* man: his body's health as well as his soul's
salvation.

"Feed on him in thy heart by faith, with thanksgiving."
Unutterable gratitude floods our hearts, making inadequate our words: "Almighty and everliving God, we
most heartily thank thee, for that thou dost vouchsafe
to feed us who have duly received these holy mysteries,

with the spiritual food of the most precious Body and Blood of thy Son our Saviour Jesus Christ."

Now, not only with our lips but with our hearts, we proclaim our praise: "Glory be to God on high . . . We praise thee, we bless thee, we worship thee, we glorify thee, we give thanks to thee for thy great glory, O Lord God, heavenly King, God the Father Almighty."

I do not profess to know or understand the full meaning of the Sacrament of Holy Communion. I know only that I have seen many evidences of its astounding healing power. I know only that through it divine grace reaches into one's very being, that the immutable truths of Christianity, inexpressible in any other way, are laid luminously bare for those who partake in faith and even partially comprehend its meaning.

"For there went virtue out of Him." Through the Sacraments, this virtue, with minimal hindrance, seems to flow into those who seek Him. But as His Spirit is not confined by space, neither is the healing ministry of the Church limited to those within its pews. By means of intercessory prayer, hundreds are being healed.

As we have previously noted, the Sacraments received by one individual, with healing intention for another, frequently result in spectacular cure for the second person, though he may be far distant from that particular Altar rail. Prayer groups meeting all over the United States are demonstrating that the power of prayer knows no boundaries. The case, for example, of a man in England miraculously healed through the prayers of a group in Baltimore, Maryland, is not exceptional.

This sort of thing, you say, is purely coincidence? I said so too, until I verified so many instances where the desperately ill and dying rallied at the exact moment of offered prayer, that it became irrational to attribute such phenomena to mere chance.

A child, comatose, temperature of 106.2, lies dying of a brain condition. Suddenly she rallies. Temperature drops, she becomes rational for the first time in seven days, sits up and asks for something to eat. The turn for the better occurred within twenty minutes of the prayers for her recovery offered by five different prayer groups.

A fifty-year-old man suffers a coronary occlusion, is rushed to the hospital and put under an oxygen tent. A group of parishioners from his church meet at 4 P.M. to pray for his recovery. At 4:10 P.M. the man rallies in spectacular fashion, and recovers. His doctor calls it a "miracle."

The wife of a man with dangerously high blood pressure asks a prayer group to meet and pray for her husband's recovery at 3 P.M. The man calls his wife at 5 P.M. to say: "About half an hour ago the strangest thing happened. The tension suddenly seemed to pour out of my body like liquid. I have the most extraordinary feeling of peace and relaxation." But he experienced this sensation at 4:30 P.M., not at 3 P.M. Why? It seems that one of the prayer group was unavoidably detained. The others waited for her. It was thus at 4:20 P.M. instead instead of 3 P.M. that they began their prayers.

These are only a few of literally hundreds of similar examples.

"Pray for one another that ye may be healed" (James 5:16). The power of intercessory and corporate prayer is pretty convincing testimony to the fact that Christianity is a fellowship and not an individual matter.

Dr. Weatherhead points out that "the powers of the Kingdom are manifested through the fellowship of the whole Church. It is the Church, not the individual, that is the extension of the Incarnation."

This being so, the Church offers us more than the teaching of Jesus. It makes available to us the incarnate life of Christ. By partaking of His Life, we know the power and the glory which is Christianity.

14

Healing Missions

THERE are a large number of religious healing movements functioning with outstanding success and making a magnificent contribution to spiritual healing. As they are too numerous for me to attempt a complete list, I would mention only a few in passing.

Within the Church, the Fellowship of St. Luke, founded by the Rev. John Gayner Banks, and the Life Abundant Movement, founded by the Rev. Robert B. H. Bell, are among the most outstanding missions of their kind. Dedicated to the quickening of the spiritual life and the restoration of the Apostolic practice of healing in the Name of Jesus Christ through prayer, anointing, and the laying-on-of-hands, they are brilliantly demonstrating that following Christ and obeying His laws brings healing to both body and soul. It is interesting to note that both these movements work in close co-operation with the medical profession, numbering among their members a sizeable group of medical doctors.

Outside the immediate realm of the Church, but adhering closely to the Church-inspired doctrine of healing, there is, among many others, the outstanding healing center in Vermont founded by two Quakers, Wallace and Rebecca Beard (E. Johnson Weaver, M.D.). Practicing group therapy through psychosomatic medicine and depth psychology, their contribution to the cause of spiritual healing is considerable. Testimony to the validity of their work lies in the fact that the ranks of their mission are being augmented continuously by members of the medical profession.

We come now to the subject of individual healers.

In the post-apostolic Church, spiritual healing was a normal part of its ministry, administered by the clergy by virtue of their office. It was also administered by certain authorized laymen possessed of a special gift of healing, such as referred to by St. Paul (I Cor. 12).

Today the same thing holds true. There are a number of laymen including Agnes Sanford, Ruth Robison, and Louise Eggleston, who are conducting marvellous personal healing missions, authorized by and closely affiliated with the Church.

The importance of keeping healing under the supervision of the Church cannot be over-emphasized. The field of non-medical healing is rife with charlatans, who with false promises of cure have hoaxed their gullible and suffering victims into parting with their last dollar and often with their lives. As Dr. Weatherhead points out, the most effective safeguard against this vicious charlatanism is for all non-clerical healers to work in co-operation with the established Church. Nevertheless, it cannot be denied that, generally speaking, the organized Church has not yet recovered the power to heal to the same extent as have a number of spiritually gifted individuals not necessarily connected with any one branch of the Church: a revivalist, for example, like Kathryn Kuhlman.

I have had occasion to investigate the Kuhlman healing

ministry carefully. I believe it to be one of the most impressive healing ministries in the world today. Not only
has her ministry of faith healed many hundreds and led
countless thousands to God, but it has inspired numerous
clergy of the organized Church to inaugurate successful
healing services in their own churches. She has done for
these men what their seminaries failed to do—taught
them how to make religion work. Through her ministry,
they have become for the first time aware of the power
of God about whom they have preached for years. They
are now translating their former lip-service into thrilling
action.

The contribution of the Kuhlman ministry to spiritual
healing has been immeasurable. In her anxiety to discover
what Christ *meant*, she has not made the all too prevalent
mistake, both in and out of the clergy, of forgetting what
He *said*. She has demonstrated the power of pure faith
and irrefutably proved the validity of Jesus' words,
preached piously for centuries, and largely unbelieved,
even by their preachers: "The works that I do shall he do
also; and greater works than these shall he do; because I
go unto the Father" (John 14:12).

But outside ministries like Kathryn Kuhlman's are
rare. Her influence, profound though it is, has necessarily been limited in its sphere; and so, also, must it be
limited in time. She will eventually die, and although her
genius has been felt by many, her great personal ministry
of healing will die with her.

The full scope and universality of spiritual healing can
only be realized through the all-embracing Christian
Church, whose influence extends to the ends of the earth
and whose ministry will go on until the end of the world.

Yet the established Church has much to learn from a ministry such as Kathryn Kuhlman's.

She has proved what appears to be an inviolable truth: regardless of healing "technique," there is only one infallible way to receive the power of Jesus Christ: keep His laws and Commandments. Dare to claim His promises, confident that "God is not a man that he should lie" (Numbers 23:19). Realize that "Without faith it is impossible to please him . . . he that cometh to God must believe that he is" (Hebrews 11:6).

Kathryn Kuhlman's teaching is orthodox and her "technique" Scripture-based and Church-founded. It is interesting to note that she makes extensive use of the system of exorcism used by Christ and carried on for centuries in the early Church: Rebuke in His Name. "In the Name of Jesus, I rebuke that illness." She knows the power in the divine Name—"which Name," we are told by early Church scholars, "cures thoroughly and effectively all who believe on Him."

That the Name of Christ actually *has* special power, may in time be scientifically confirmed by means of radiaesthesia. This is a new branch of science still in the experimental stage, which deals with a method of analytical diagnosis of disease, based on the measurements of wave lengths emanating from the human body. Recent reports from researchers reveal an astounding fact: the Name of Jesus and the sign of the Cross affect to a marked degree radiation coming from the body.

Those who are commendably searching for better and more effective healing "technique" will observe that Kathryn Kuhlman propounds no new dogmatic tenets and promulgates no revolutionary theories. She merely stands firm as the Rock of Peter upon her unalterable conviction that Christ meant exactly what He said.

She makes no attempt at involved theological interpretation, but accepts at face value His promise: "And all things, whatsoever ye shall ask in prayer, believing, ye shall receive." The effectiveness of her ministry is proof of the validity of its premise.

Lest any of us be led astray by our enthusiasm for a ministry such as Kathryn Kuhlman's, it is well to remember that such geniuses of the spirit are few and far between. The usual evangelistic healing mission is fraught with danger, subject to the most flagrant abuses.

Fortunately, as the healing ministry within the Church has grown, we are no longer dependent for guidance and inspiration on the infrequent genius of a few great independent healers. We need no longer seek salvation or healing from uncertain sources. We may find now, within the orthodox Church, that which we seek—the living God. Here there is no room for charlatans. Spiritual healing flows uncorrupted and uncontaminated from its Source.

There are now clergymen in nearly every branch of the Church possessed of outstanding healing gifts: men like Episcopalian Alfred Price, Baptist Roland Brown, and Methodist Albert Day. But we need not rely solely on specialists in their field, for as Agnes Sanford points out, the gift of healing is conferred upon every Episcopal priest at his ordination. "Receive the Holy Ghost . . . be thou a faithful Dispenser of the Word of God, and of his holy Sacraments" (Book of Common Prayer, p. 546).

Every ordained priest has at hand those tools for healing of body and soul, bequeathed us by Jesus Christ, sanctified by His Spirit, brightened by rediscovered knowledge, and reanimated by a revived expectant faith. No priest of himself can add to or detract from the life-giving, soul-saving power of the Sacraments when they are properly understood and received in true faith.

It seems clear that no one branch of the Church and no one individual healer can hold the complete answer to spiritual healing. This must ultimately be found in the Church Universal which was divinely commissioned by Him, through His Apostles, to carry on His work. A Church unified by faith in Christ's total redemptive ministry can demonstrate, to its fullest extent, the endless mercy and the boundless power of the Holy Spirit of which it is chief custodian.

Through the ministry of spiritual healing, we catch a vision of an undivided Church striding mightily forward, invincible in its strength and unlimited in its spiritual power.

We have seen the remarkable evidence of God's power released by the faith of one individual. We have seen the incredible results evoked by the corporate faith of a few thousands. When the Churches of Christ, embracing Christians all over the world, unite in a common faith in His healing power, we will know a force which will change the course of the world.

15

Lourdes

NO DISCUSSION of spiritual healing would be complete without mention of Lourdes.

Since 1858, when the little peasant girl, Bernadette, alleged that she saw repeated visions of the Virgin Mary, thousands from all over the world have claimed miraculous healings by the Holy Waters there.

A typical year finds as many as three million pilgrims on their way to the French town, accompanied by some fifteen hundred doctors of every faith or none, who go to observe and record what they have seen.

What is the truth? Is Lourdes a cruel hoax, the mecca, not of healing, but of heartbreak, for the incredibly gullible? Are the reported cures not true healings, but only psychological manifestations induced by religious hysteria?

I think not. I believe that an objective study of the scientific evidence relating to Lourdes' healings, undertaken without prejudice or bigotry, reveals that these miraculous healings cannot be lightly dismissed as the inconsequential results of mass hysteria or religious fanaticism.

It was in 1903 that Dr. Alexis Carrel first traveled to Lourdes to observe at first hand, in his capacity as scientist, the reported phenomena.

Open-minded, but admittedly skeptical, he was to say to the priest in charge, "If God exists, miracles (of healing) are possible. But does God exist? All I can say is that no miracle has ever yet been scientifically observed. To the scientific mind, a miracle is an absurdity. To convince me that miracles exist, I would have to see an organic disease cured—a cancer disappearing—a congenital dislocation suddenly vanishing. I assure you that if I actually saw one single wound close and heal before my eyes, I would either become a fanatic or go mad."

In a position to examine patients, and with the authority to study in detail their case histories, the young doctor was to witness the scientifically impossible. He was to see a cancer wither and die before his eyes. He was to see a woman whom he knew to be at the point of death from advanced tuberculous peritonitis instantly and miraculously restored.

Dr. Carrel did not go mad, nor did he become a fanatic. He later became a surgeon of renown and a winner of the Nobel prize for physiology and medicine. But his entire life was profoundly affected by what he had witnessed at Lourdes. He was later to write: "The influence of prayer on the human mind and body is as demonstrable as that of secreting glands. Prayer, like radium, is a source of luminous, self-generating energy; whenever we address God in fervent prayer, we change both body and soul for the better."

The young doctor's report on Lourdes was perhaps the first to deal with the phenomena with unemotional, scientific detachment. A doubting non-Catholic world was stirred into its first tentative credence.

During the past fifty years, the Roman Catholic Church

has been unable to prevent the crass commercialism of the small town of Lourdes—an unfortunate fact, for many observers are so unfavorably impressed that they cannot see the spiritual forest because of the materialistic trees. But it is there, if one has the patience to look beyond human weakness to the great spiritual forces which are in operation at the site of the Holy Waters.

The Roman Church has taken extraordinary precautions to safeguard the religious reputation of Lourdes, and to guarantee the validity of each claimed miracle.

A medical board, comprised of physicians of every faith and of impeccable integrity, has been established for the specific purpose of investigating alleged healings. So rigorous is the scientific scrutiny, so irrefutable are the medical findings, that unless one is blinded by bigotry and intolerance, the authenticity of the healings cannot, in my opinion, be reasonably questioned. This judgment is upheld by any informed medical men who have taken the time and trouble to investigate.

The medical bureau begins by automatically barring from miracle status any cures which might conceivably be due to hysteria or other psychological factors. This precludes from consideration thousands of alleged healings of lameness, paralysis, certain types of blindness, and numerous other ailments which fall into the category of possible psychological cure.

Before a healing is accepted as miraculous, certain adamant conditions must be met.

(1) The normal time factor of healing must have been dramatically and indisputably shortened. That is to say, a cancer must have instantly disappeared; a suppurating

wound must have spontaneously closed; a congenital dislocation must have suddenly disappeared.

(2) There must be no relapses. For this reason, no miracle is accepted as such unless it has been observed over a period of years.

(3) Following the healing, every clinical feature of the disease which formerly existed must be removed.

In connection with this last condition, Dr. Woodard relates an interesting case, similar to one I have reported in an earlier chapter. Three years before the doctor's journey to Lourdes, a woman had visited the shrine, seeking healing for a completely fixed spine, due to advanced ankylotic spondylitis. One day, while praying at the Grotto, her back suddenly became mobile. She was taken at once to the *Bureau de Médecin*, where another set of X-rays was immediately made. The case was *not* officially accepted as a miracle, because the X-rays still showed advanced disease of the spine.

"Yet," says the physician, "what was there to explain the fact which I saw with my own eyes—that she could bend down and pick up anything off the floor without the slightest pain or difficulty? It is all very well to say that for the reputation of Lourdes such a case cannot be accepted as a miracle, but science has no explanation as yet of how she was able to do it." This was clearly another of those cases of which I have seen many: scientifically impossible, they exist.

It is certainly true, however, that despite the many remarkable cures, the majority seeking healing at Lourdes are disappointed. Why?

Based on what I have learned of spiritual healing, the reasons seem pretty clear. If Lourdes is a citadel of the faithful, it has also become a mecca for the superstitious. Thousands of all faiths and none, who make the pilgrimage, go not with the faith that it is the will of God to heal them, but in the belief that the waters themselves possess some weird and magic curative power. Like Caligula who believed that there was some strange necromancy in the Master's robe, thousands of Lourdes' pilgrims believe that there is a mystical enchantment in the shrine itself. They are unaware that the ritual of immersion in Holy Water is no substitute for the repentance not sought; nor can a superstitious belief in a pool of water compensate for lack of true faith in the love and power of God to heal. Some have estimated that only 2% of those who seek healing at Lourdes are rewarded.

Yet while it is true that the Lourdes Medical Commission has accepted as miracles only fifty-one among thousands of alleged cures, this infinitesimal number of officially accepted miracles does not present a valid picture of Lourdes. Moral and psychic cures, as well as those for nervous disorders, undoubtedly number in the thousands. Then there are numerous cases which, although not explicable in scientific terms, fail, for one reason or another, to meet the rigid conditions established by the medical board.

Take, for example, the man who had come to Lourdes obviously in the final stages of advanced tuberculosis. Healed, he returned to the shrine several years later, looking well and active. His case was rejected because of incomplete records. Or take the case of a small girl who had been crippled from birth, who suddenly walked. Her case was rejected on the grounds that the cure might have been psychological.

There are numerous cases which, although they would appear to meet the rigid requirements of the Bureau of Medical Findings, are never submitted to the authorities: many because the obligation to return to Lourdes a year later cannot be fulfilled; many more because if the patient is healed, he too often has no interest whatsoever in submitting his case to a medical court to be assured of what he already knows—that he is now well.

I have discovered in the preparation of this book that the vast majority of those spiritually healed take the attitude: "I have been healed by the power of God. That is all I know and all I need to know." The fact of his healing suffices, and he feels, with some justification, that he does not need scientific evidence to prove what he himself knows to be a fact. Those healed at Lourdes are no exception to the general rule.

While this disinterest in scientific verification may be understandable, it is, in my judgment, incalculably detrimental to the cause of spiritual healing. Personal knowledge of one's own healing may suffice for that individual, but once touched by the healing hand of Christ, those healed have an obligation far beyond a personal acceptance of our Lord. They are His stewards, whose duty it is to quicken the moribund belief of others all over the world. They are proselytes of the faith that He still lives. They are promulgators of the knowledge that His will for us is good.

Their witness of His power must be couched in terms understood and acceptable to twentieth-century skeptical, scientifically-disposed intellects, which means that it must include, wherever possible, concrete scientific evidence of the validity of their healings.

By their witness they must make crystal clear that they are not hysterics, wishful thinkers, or religious fanatics, but only run-of-the-mine Christians, who have dared to claim His promise. They must offer themselves as scientifically demonstrable proof that He lives and that "to them that believe, signs will follow." They are the apostles of the twentieth century.

Regardless of miraculous healings, there is at Lourdes one of the most extraordinary and significant evidences of the living Presence of Christ in the world today. The evidence lies in the waters of the pool.

The modern doctor contemplates with horror the unhygienic prospect of hundreds of the sick bathing in the seldom changed waters. Many suffer contagious diseases; many are incontinent; scores have running sores and suppurating wounds. How much disease, then, is transmitted in the almost stagnant water? The answer is—none—and herein lies perhaps the greatest miracle of all.

Never, since 1858, has there been recorded a single case of transferred infection, a fact which violates every known law of hygiene. At one time action was threatened to close the baths on hygienic grounds. Three thousand *doctors* immediately protested.

Repeated scientific experiments have proved that all microbes instantly lose their virulence as soon as they come in contact with the Lourdes waters.

A Naples doctor has demonstrated conclusively that animals infected with microbes subjected to Lourdes waters do not develop disease, but similar animals infected with the same microbes subjected to ordinary river water die in a few days.

The average conscientious doctor shudders at the pros-

pect of the desperately sick undergoing the rigors of a
Lourdes pilgrimage. If by some chance they should arrive
at their destination still alive, he trembles at the madness
which makes them further jeopardize their lives by plung-
ing into not only contaminated, but cold, water.

The doctor's fears are groundless. The infectious element aside, it is interesting to note that there is no record
of any harm ever having come to anyone, regardless of his
condition, by immersion in the Holy Waters.

But what of these so-called "records," you may well be
thinking. Are they not the biased reports of the religious?
No. They are compiled, examined, and verified by medical
men from all over the world, men of every faith, believers
and skeptics, who have one thing in common: their scientific accuracy and integrity.

"We have never known," reports Dr. Francois Leuret,
"a case to be worse after a bath. Heart cases, tuberculosis
victims, the dying are all plunged into the waters, and all
of them stand the experience without complications and
without fatigue. . . . Here is a phenomenon beyond medical
reasoning; this is what I call the continual miracle which
cannot be explained by science and which is outside the
normal laws of hygiene."

In view of the remarkable factors associated with the
Lourdes waters, is there not, then, inherent in them, some
actual healing power?

From the scientific viewpoint, the water gushing from
the spring contains no discernible therapeutic agent. Repeated chemical analyses have proved it to be neither more
nor less than good drinking water.

That there is no special healing virtue in the water itself
comes as no surprise to the student of spiritual healing,

nor should it surprise the student of the Lourdes phenomena, for there is ample evidence that as many are healed
in the religious processions and at Mass at the French shrine
as are cured by bathing in the pool.

It would seem indisputable that the powerful healing
factor present at Lourdes lies not in some supposed magic
inherent in its Holy Waters nor in a peculiar concentration
of the Holy Spirit at the shrine. It is the result of the ex-
pressions of *active* faith which the pilgrimage itself denotes
when it is undertaken in the spirit of true religious belief
quickened to the heights of expectancy by immersion in the
Holy Waters.

Much the same factor was present in the healing of the
Biblical Lydia. You will remember that she stretched out
her hand and touched the hem of the Master's garment
and was healed. Does this imply that there was some
mysterious healing virtue in the cloth of His robe? No. It
was Lydia's openly expressed act of faith which our Lord
recognized and honored by healing her.

So it is at Lourdes—and so, incidentally, is it at any
church healing service. Your presence there signifies an
active expression of faith.

Christ is with you always, wherever you are. You don't
have to go to Lourdes or even to your own church to be
healed by Him. But in the special way in which His
Presence is real at Holy Communion, so is His power
uniquely abundant before the massed faith of expectant
believers, gathered together in a sign of active faith. He
has promised that when two or three are gathered together
in His Name, He will grant our requests. He fulfills that
promise.

In view of the millions who flock to Lourdes, the number

of physical healings occurring there is far from impressive. Perhaps this is because more believe in the curative powers of the water than in the love of God; more seek healing in the name of comfort than in the name of Christ. Nevertheless, this is a great shrine, illumined by the incontrovertible evidence of God's Presence, and hallowed by the prayers of millions of the truly faithful.

As we become increasingly aware of the truth that the power of the living God is available to all who, in expectant faith, seek healing in His Name; as the organized Church grows in the faith and knowledge that God can and does heal all disease; as Christians everywhere unite in the unassailable conviction that God truly lives, saving us by His infinite compassion, healing us by His limitless power, protecting us by His incalculable might, and strengthening us by His inestimable love, the ultimate miracle may yet come to pass. The world itself may become as the pool at Lourdes, purified by faith and hallowed by His Presence with all evil rendered impotent and harmless by His almighty power.

16

Christian Science and Spiritual Healing

SO MANY people have asked me what, if any, is the difference between Christian Science and spiritual healing; so many have said, "Why aren't you a Christian Scientist if you believe in non-medical cures?" that it seems worthwhile to summarize briefly the differences between the two healing methods.

Perhaps the most fundamental difference between Christian Science and spiritual healing lies in their antithetical approach to the subjects of sin, evil, and disease, which stems from an irreconcilable difference in theological tenets.

Christian Science proceeds from the basis that, as God is all-good, nothing *except* God has any reality. Therefore, it follows that sin, evil, and disease, being contrary to the nature of God, are mere illusion.

"Human mind and body are myths," says Mary Baker Eddy, founder of the movement. For the Christian Scientist, therefore, sin, evil, and disease do not exist.

The Church, on the other hand, recognizes the existence of sin and evil and disease as concrete forces opposing God's will. When, for example, we see a man writhing in pain, we do not deny the existence of the cancer which is eating away his vital organs. We openly acknowledge it as a dreadful reality, emanating not from God, but from an evil source. We combat it, not by ignoring its existence, but by fighting it with God's greater power. We seek to realize this power by removing its most obvious obstruction—our own sin.

While we believe that physical healing is important, the end-all of our religion is not the curing of some of the body's ailments. It is primarily the soul's salvation, the being brought to God, which, if we are to believe our Saviour, depends on two things: repentance and faith. "Repent ye and believe," He said in no uncertain terms. Therefore, it is our Christ-based conviction that "If we say that we have no sin, we deceive ourselves, and the truth is not in us."

The underlying philosophy of Christian Science is un- tenable to the orthodox Christian, but if we are going to be honest, we will have to admit that the success, indeed the very existence, of the Christian Science movement is attributable to the shortcomings of the orthodox Church.

Dr. John Gayner Banks, one of this country's great leaders in spiritual healing, points out that "the modern healing movement, as we know it, started some seventy- five years ago with the publication of *Science and Health,* by Mary Baker Eddy."

Critics may disparage the over-emphasis of Christian Science on physical healings (and it is a strange paradox that their denial of the reality of matter so often results in a fixed concentration on that which they deny exists), but the fact remains, as Dr. Banks goes on to say, that the Church's *under*-emphasis on healing for so many centuries is doubtless responsible for the over-reaction of the Scientist toward physical health. It seems apparent that had the Church retained its once powerful healing ministry, Christian Science would never have come into being, for it is a religion determined by man's desire for a healthy body. The Church should have continued to fulfil this vital need.

There is a wide divergence of opinion between the two schools of healing on the subject of the medical profession. Although Mary Baker Eddy declared, ". . . it is better for Christian Scientists to leave surgery and the adjustment of broken bones and dislocations to the fingers of a surgeon," the vast majority of practicing Scientists are adamantly opposed to consulting doctors. To do so, they feel, might cast a reflection on the caliber of their faith. If ill, the Scientist attempts to attain metaphysical healing through prayer and study of his textbook, *Science and Health*. If his own efforts fail, he calls in a practitioner trained in the tenets of metaphysics as set forth by Mrs. Eddy. By changing the patient's mental attitude, remarkable cures are effected, for the power of mind over matter can no longer be disputed.

Many doctors claim—and Mary Baker Eddy upholds this claim—that of every hundred cases of illness, fifty would recover if left untended; and of the remaining fifty, twenty-five are of psychosomatic origin. In the remaining twenty-five cases, Christian Science often gets results. Its failures, however, have occasioned numerous Scientists to abandon their religion with the bitter words: "I have seen too many die."

The healing ministry of the Church, proceeding on the theory that God gave us minds to use, and that knowledge is of God and therefore good, urges a close co-operation between spiritual healing and medical science.

"Honour a physician . . . for the Lord hath created him. The Lord hath created medicines out of the earth; and he that is wise will not abhor them" (Ecclesiasticus 38:1, 4).

Evelyn Frost, Ph.D., accurately sums up the viewpoint of the Church towards medicine when she writes: "The fact that the healing may be mediated through Christians within the medical profession does not alter the conclusion that the healing has its origin in Christ. . . . It is characteristic of His working that He uses fully what man has to offer. . . ."

It is the failure to recognize this that accounts for those tragedies in Christian Science, concerning which Dr. Weatherhead comments: "Co-operation with the medical profession would not lessen the cures of Christian Science, but it would lessen the number of disasters which happen through its unintelligent application."

There are those who claim that Christian Science is a false nomenclature, as it is neither Christian nor science. While it is true that the movement is neither conventionally Christian nor scientific in the usual sense, it contains elements of both. It is a metaphysical (the science of being) method of healing based, if not on orthodox Christianity, at least on certain vital and dynamic Christian principles.

Through its employment of metaphysical methods, it has achieved some startling demonstrations of the power of mind over matter. It is Christian in principle because of its recognition of the power of God, in its concern with things eternal rather than temporal, and in its emphasis on love.

"God is love; there are no qualifications or mental reservations to that affirmation," says Dr. Alfred Price, and this is the principle on which Mary Baker Eddy founded her movement. "Divine love," she states, "has met and always will meet human need."

In its unequivocal teaching of God's love and will for

humanity, Christian Science has made an inestimable contribution to Christianity. According to the orthodox Church, the movement may be heretic, but in fairness we must note that it refutes one of the greatest of all heresies, the more monstrous because Church-taught: the heresy that sickness is God's will for us, sent as direct punishment for our sins.

Many orthodox Christians still expound this heresy; they are still convinced that saintliness is irrevocably linked with sickness, while the mark of a good Christian is the stern countenance with thin lips drawn tight with suffering.

We cannot deny that Christian Science has recaptured the all but lost Christian joy. The radiant face and serene eyes of the average Scientist are testimony that he has hold of something which too many of the rest of us have not been able to find.

Although denying the reality of matter and emphasizing the spiritual nature of man to the extent that the human body is dismissed as a myth; although based on a philosophy essentially alien to the Gospels, Christian Science has yet curiously managed to revive, in some respects, the New Testament conception of the body as an honored temple of the Holy Spirit, undefiled and perfect.

Why, then, am I not a Scientist? For many reasons.

I cannot deny the reality of the flesh, for if I do, I deny Christ, who is God in the flesh.

I cannot deny the reality of pain, for if I do, I deny Christianity as I understand it, on the authority of its Founder, Jesus Christ. "And Christ suffered." A basic premise of Christianity is that our Saviour *suffered* in expiation for our sins. If I deny suffering, then I deny the

Atonement. If I deny sin, I deny my redemption. If I deny the Personality of God, I deny the Incarnation. If I deny His real death on the Cross, I deny the Resurrection.

In short, I cannot deny the reality of evil and sin and pain, for if I do, I must deny our Lord.

My knowledge of Jesus Christ comes to me from the Gospels. They tell me that Jesus healed the sick who came to Him; that He recognized their disease as evil and rebuked it; that He made them well, not of illusory disabilities, but of all too real afflictions.

I believe that the doctrine of the resurrection of the body is what differentiates Christianity from all other religions. When Christ appeared to His Disciples, He did not glide out of the ether as a nebulous, unidentifiable spirit. He came to them in recognizable form. "The saved man is a *complete* man," said Irenaeus. St. Paul was his authority: "I pray God your whole spirit and soul and body be preserved blameless unto the coming of our Lord Jesus Christ" (I Thess. 5:23).

I believe in what I consider Christianity's greatest gift to me—a personal relationship with God through Jesus Christ. I am starved and repelled by the cold remoteness of Infinite Mind.

I believe that pain is a reality which can be, in Christ's Name, transcended. As Dr. Price says, "They who would rob us of the reality of pain, rob us of the reality of triumph."

I believe that sin and evil are realities which can be overcome by the power of God only if we acknowledge, not ignore, their existence.

I believe that the Sacraments, as instituted by Christ, are

the means of grace, which, opening the channels to Him, enable us to realize our hope of glory.

I believe that medical science is a gift of God, as surely as the earth's fertile fields. To permit either to lie fallow in a needy world is, in my opinion, contrary to His will.

These are some of the reasons why I could not be a Scientist. Nevertheless, taking into full account the theological quicksand on which Christian Science is founded, there are important philosophical and psychological truths inherent in the movement which I believe the orthodox Church could adopt with benefit.

As Dr. Weatherhead points out: "The Christian Scientists confuse us when they talk of pain having no reality, but they are right in denying it the same kind of reality as health. For health is something which ought to be. Disease is something which ought not to be. It cannot have the positive reality of good, for as God's will is done, it will be excluded and will disappear, while health or wholeness abides forever."

Much of the healing success of Christian Science can be attributed to the utilization of elementary psychological principles acknowledged for years by the medical profession. Sick emotions breed sick bodies; pessimism, hate, revenge, and above all, fear, are devastating to good health; to turn a sick person's mind away from his own suffering is always beneficial. We know now that to turn it toward the face of God can accomplish miracles.

Christian Science's record of cures and the manifest love, joy, and obvious freedom from fear of most of its adherents constitute a challenge to those orthodox Churches which still maintain the heresy that agony is the will of God.

If Christian Science tends to confuse the power of mind

over matter with the kind of healing Christ did and commanded His Church to continue in His Name; if it tends to regard bodily health as the main goal of its faith rather than a by-product of man's relationship with God; if it weakens its own cause by the same hostility to medical science which virtually destroyed the healing ministry of the Early Church, it is nevertheless true that "The very same basic truth which underlies metaphysical healing, taken into the Church, purified by the doctrine of the Incarnation, and made available through the Christian Sacraments, would give the Church incredible power in the propagation of its great message" (John Gayner Banks).

17

Doctors Look at Spiritual Healing

IN AN EFFORT to gain some insight into the medical profession's attitude toward spiritual healing, I have contacted doctors all over the United States.

There is little doubt that the majority of physicians believe in God. "Show me the doctor who denies the existence of the Supreme Being," says Dr. Elmer Hess, President of the American Medical Association, "and I will say that he has no right to practice the healing art."

But regardless of belief in God, it would be a gross misstatement of fact to imply that the medical profession as a whole is either aware of or interested in spiritual healing as such. I am impressed, however, by the growing number of physicians who, over a very brief period of time, have become not only interested in the subject, but fully accept its basic premise: complete health of the individual is a triune affair, depending not only on healing of the body and mind, but on healing of the spirit as well.

"In the past," declares a prominent west coast doctor, "we have not looked for the disease of the spirit, but have been satisfied with a physical or mental diagnosis. We are now coming to realize more and more that physical healings, while important, are not complete until there is also the healing of the spirit."

Only a few years ago, a statement of this sort would have labeled a physician a "crackpot" or a medical renegade. Today it signifies the growing realization of the medical profession that good health is more than a problem of the body and mind. As the Church, with the revival of spiritual healing, has become "health" conscious, so is the doctor becoming conscious of the importance of the spirit.

This rather revolutionary change of medical attitude seems, paradoxically, to be the result of modern scientific achievement. The renascence of divine healing has occurred simultaneously with spectacular progress in medical science. Not only is the doctor as a scientist inclined now to eliminate the word "impossible" from his vocabulary, but new knowledge of psychosomatics has extended the horizons of medicine far beyond the old confines of drugs and surgery.

Through the advancement of psychosomatic medicine, the importance of treating the individual rather than the disease has been generally recognized. The close interrelationship of body, mind, and emotions is no longer mere supposition; it is established fact. According to the Mayo Clinic, 50% of disease is due to emotional disturbance. A recent survey estimates that more than half of those admitted to hospitals are not really medical, but mental and spiritual cases. They may, and usually do, suffer from serious physical complaints, but doctors have reported that their fundamental need is mental wholeness and true religion. Research conducted in accident cases indicates that 85% of accidents occur to 15% of our people and these 15% are, in general, emotionally disturbed.

The list of so-called "stress" diseases continues to grow. It already includes, among others, rheumatoid arthritis, asthma, duodenal ulcers, ulcerative colitis, hypertension, and a variety of heart ailments. "Some," says surgeon Sir Heneage Ogilvie, "would add diabetes in younger people."

Cancer may be next on the list. Dr. Eugene Blumfield, directing research at the Veterans' Administration Hospital at Long Beach, California, states that most of those who seem to possess exceptional resistance to cancer growth are people who have learned to "avoid or reduce excessive emotional stress."

Psychosomatics, then, is the bridge between medicine and spiritual healing. More and more doctors are daring to cross it, for they are learning that no one facet of the individual stands in isolation from the other. "Disease concerns the total personality," comments a medical man, "and therefore the treatment must be total in aspect: medical, psychiatric, and spiritual."

Today's accepted medical procedure of treating the mind and emotions in order to heal the body of what only a short time back was considered purely physical disease, has undeniably given impetus to the concept that the spirit, as an integral part of man, must be treated if complete healing is to occur.

A well-known California doctor observes: "As we are constantly adding to the list of physical ailments which are due to the mind, more and more of us are beginning to believe that the instigating cause of all illness is spiritual."

The average physician has long been aware that he is not responsible for the actual healing process. In fact, at the beginning of the century, medical students were taught to be sure to do nothing with a patient which might interfere with his natural recovery! Medical opinion seems unanimously agreed that there is in existence a healing factor which is outside the sphere of medical science. A few doctors term this factor an "unseen force," with no discernible theological connection, but a preponderant number attribute healing to the Supreme Being. Many doctors, through faith and prayer, are releasing that healing power which they are convinced comes directly from God.

"We know more medicine than ever before in history," a young physician remarked to me recently, "but we are also keenly aware of our limitations. We can only minister to the sick with our material tools of medicine. God must do the rest. We've known for a long time that the most responsive patients are those with a deep religious faith. Now we're beginning to see that the most successful doctors are those who practice prayer as well as medicine in their treatment of disease."

Some doctors will admit that spiritual healing is a "brilliantly effective" means of psychotherapy, but beyond this they will not go. However, a prominent physician, himself healed of a congenital bone displacement, asks: "Since when has psychotherapy cured congenital disease? When I see the results of spiritual healing, I can't help but wonder if I've been in the wrong profession all these years."

I have interviewed a number of doctors who openly sneer at spiritual healing and, regardless of evidence, continue their loud chant of "wrong diagnosis." But I have also observed that many of those whose voices a few years ago would have been heard above the rest now echo, instead, the words of Dr. Alexis Carrel: "As a physician, I have seen men, after all other therapy had failed, lifted out of disease and melancholy by the serene effort of prayer.

It is the only power in the world that seems to overcome the so-called 'laws of nature.'"

I have been surprised at the number of doctors who send their patients to attend healing services, some even sitting in the pews with those seeking healing. Many of these men could, like Dr. Seymour Price, "testify to cases, both personal and professional, where spiritual healing has wrought results which would convince the most skeptical." But most are still reluctant to have their names publicly associated with divine healing. Why? A physician, himself healed by prayer after medicine had failed, gives a typical explanation: "To the majority of people, laymen and doctors alike, spiritual healing is a strange, new concept. If I permitted my name to be quoted, those of my patients who knew nothing of the subject would immediately jump to the conclusion that I was 'off my rocker.' The A.M.A. would doubtless contend that a physician who advocated 'faith' healing had no business practicing medicine. I'd be through as a doctor, and unfortunately I have to eat!"

Nevertheless, there is no longer any hesitancy among doctors in proclaiming the efficacy of religion as a healing influence. The vast majority frankly concede that drugs and surgery are not the final answer to healing, nor is psychotherapy alone a cure-all for psychosomatic disease.

"I have found," says a doctor with a very large practice, "that unless there is a spiritual change in the patient, his cure is not likely to be permanent. The one disease will be cured, but almost invariably, another one follows."

A specialist, probably the most eminent man in the world in his particular field, urges his colleagues to distinguish between the mind and the spirit. Psychotherapy, although invaluable, tends to be more of a palliative than a cure.

Just as insulin enables a diabetic to live with his disease without curing it, so mental therapy endeavors to teach a disturbed person to adjust to those evil conditions which caused his sickness. The evil itself is not removed.

The reaction of the majority of doctors when confronted for the first time with the subject of spiritual healing is one of immediate antagonism. In every case with which I am personally familiar, this hostility has proved to be due to a total misunderstanding of the aims and purposes of the ministry of healing. When doctors realize that the Church in no way opposes medicine, they are the first to acknowledge the benefits of a co-operative and united ministry for healing of both body and soul.

It is significant that there is the most active co-operation between clergy and doctors in those areas where the healing ministry is most widespread. Here the physician has the opportunity to see the healing clergy at work. In a position to observe the frequently dramatic benefits derived from this unity of treatment, he is impressed, often in spite of himself. He is not prepared to publicly proclaim unexpected healings as miracles, but he is frank in his acknowledgement that the Church is a powerful ally in the treatment of the sick.

One doctor on the staff of a large hospital comments: "I had my first experience with the healing clergy some two years ago. The minister visited an ill patient just prior to an extremely serious operation. Immediately following the laying-on-of-hands, a distinct improvement in the patient's condition was noted—not only mentally and spiritually, but physically. Curiously, the operation proved far less serious than we had anticipated, and the patient's recovery was unusually rapid and complete. I have seen this same thing happen so many times now, that I not only urge my patients to seek spiritual help, but I, too, seek this help before undertaking serious surgery."

"But the clergy have *always* ministered to the sick," you say. "What do they do now that is so different?" The chief difference lies in the fact that today the clergy come not merely to console, but to heal.

"I shudder to think of my former prayers of quick resignation," says a clergyman who three years ago instituted what has become an outstandingly effective healing ministry. "I have learned now to claim the promises of Christ with boldness."

Medical men are justly concerned and rightfully cautious that a patient should not jeopardize his health and life by refusing indicated medical treatment. When they comprehend the principles underlying divine healing, they realize that the clergy are not charlatans; those who seek healing from God are not irrational fanatics, but Christians who recognize that healing is mediated by God through many diverse channels, which include the Church, the psychologist, and the physician.

"He hath given men skill, that he might be honoured in his marvellous works. With such doth he heal men, and taketh away their pains" (Ecclesiasticus 38:6-7).

Because the average doctor agrees with the clergyman that all actual healing is, in truth, divine, he is, with increasing frequency, admonishing his patients to ". . . pray unto the Lord, and he will make thee whole" (Ecclesiasticus 38:9).

As time goes on, more and more clergymen are able to say, as does the rector of a large Presbyterian church: "The most encouraging sign of all is that our best friends are physicians, who count us as true allies and helpers, and not as competitors."

Many individuals have learned to seek God's healing power in co-operation with medicine. A great many more wait until medicine has failed. It should not be that so many of us place our faith in Christ as a last resort, but human nature being as it is, we will doubtless continue for a long time to come to try first the "easy" way of medicine alone. For spiritual healing is far from easy for the average person. The acquisition of real faith, the honest confession of our sins, the truly contrite heart, the utter relinquishment of self and pride—these things are incredibly difficult, as is all of Christianity. No doctor need fear that medicine will soon be forsaken, for regardless of any teaching on the subject, it is so infinitely less demanding upon us to sit passively in a doctor's office, than to kneel with active faith in a church pew!

If, as so many physicians are now convinced, the optimum health of the patient depends on co-operation between medicine and religion, what is necessary for sufficient medical endorsement to make such co-operation widespread—the general rule and not the exception? I believe the answer hinges on one factor: the proper compilation of detailed and exact records.

The average clergyman has not sensed, until very recently, the importance of exact records. For him, as for the patient, the fact that healing occurred was sufficient. He has felt, also, and with considerable justification, that no matter what the evidence, the die-hard skeptic would refuse to believe.

A prominent New York psychiatrist, who practices prayer along with his psychiatry, and has seen a number of medically "hopeless" psychotics restored to health, seems to corroborate the clerical viewpoint when he comments, "The skeptic's disbelief is not intellectual. I feel that his disbelief is on a subconscious level—and subconscious mind is not subject to the laws of reason."

I take minor issue with this statement, feeling that it should be qualified to apply chiefly to one type of skeptic —the individual who, arrogant in his disbelief, blinded by prejudice and hostility, is clearly impervious to reason or evidence. But there is also the man whose skepticism is like that of the good scientist. He harbors a rational, honest doubt. He will disbelieve only until such time as sufficient trustworthy evidence is offered that will change his mind. And finally there is the man of great latent faith who has in his heart the desire to believe, but cannot because the evidence which will convince him intellectually is lacking. It is my opinion that most people fit into one or the other of these last two categories. It is for them that a sufficient accumulation of properly compiled and detailed documentation should be procured.

It is clearly impossible for a doctor, no matter how keenly interested, to devote, as I have had to, many months to ferreting out the numerous obscure medical backgrounds and difficult-to-obtain records of those who claim divine healing. There is, to be sure, an abundance of filed case histories, but in the main, these are not thoroughly scientifically documented. The existing files of a comparatively few widely-scattered doctors, however complete the records, do not comprise the massive *cumulative* evidence required. On the basis of what is readily available, it is too easy for the skeptic to claim "wrong diagnosis" or "sheer coincidence."

Happily, steps are now being taken to remedy the inadequacy of the records. At a recent seminar on spiritual healing, it was agreed that a uniform method of recording cases should be put into effect immediately. Towards this end, Dr. Frank Sladen of the Henry Ford Hospital in Detroit, Michigan, has devised a form record blank which makes provision for all pertinent data such as medical diagnosis, method of diagnosis, laboratory reports, and full details of spiritual healing with corroborative medical evidence.

As this type of scientific documentation accumulates and as it becomes more readily accessible and easily available to the medical profession for study, it will become increasingly difficult to deny the reality of God's healing power, and the cries of "wrong diagnosis" will gradually fade into oblivion.

When someone asked Dr. James Bell, M.D., what he considered his greatest discovery, he answered, "The fact that I was a sinner and Jesus Christ my Saviour." There is abundant evidence that this may prove the greatest over-all medical discovery of our century.

18

Physics and Spiritual Healing

I HAVE found that the skeptical layman and the scientist usually share a common initial reaction when first confronted with the subject of spiritual healing. They shrug their shoulders, and with a muttered "impossible" they proceed to ignore the entire matter.

However, after discussing spiritual healing in detail with a large number of both uninitiated laymen and competent scientists, I have made an interesting discovery: once he has been prevailed upon to listen, the scientist is a lot easier to convince than the doubting layman. This is not as surprising as it might seem.

Most of us today are inclined to be over-imbued with scientific fervor. We approach the subject of miraculous healing with skepticism, which is as it should be. We want the truth, and we should be wary of being "taken in." However, the pseudo-scientific attitude we assume is a far cry from the true scientific approach. In the hallowed names of Reason and Science, we repudiate, without analysis, an idea which appears to us as unprovable, irrational, and thus highly unscientific. We flatly deny the healing phenomenon because, in our estimation, it is manifestly "impossible." So complete is our rejection that we refuse even to consider the evidence presented, let alone study it. Our refusal to examine any facts which do not fit neatly into our preconceived theories indelibly marks us as scientifically uninformed laymen. The true scientist is never guilty of thus placing the cart before the horse. He meticulously observes a cardinal rule of all research: make your theories fit the facts.

He approaches the subject with the unbiased objectivity which has made possible all scientific discovery. He is intensely reluctant to consider anything "impossible." He stands ready to meet the challenge of the unexpected and the currently inexplicable. He is trained to consider and evaluate all available evidence. If it appears conclusive, he is prepared to accept it as a working hypothesis until it is disproved by the discovery of new evidence to the contrary.

It occurs to the scientist, as it does not to the layman, that it may be the inadequacy of today's scientific knowledge to explain it, rather than the phenomenon itself, which places miraculous healing in the realm of the incredible.

No one is more fully aware of the limitations of his own knowledge than the scientist. "I have never heard so many people say 'I don't know,'" reported Edward R. Murrow after visiting the Princeton Institute of Advanced Study of which Dr. J. Robert Oppenheimer is Director.

Dr. Oppenheimer is the first to acknowledge that "everything that is known to man is known only in a very sketchy way. Things that are thought by a man to be relevant and exciting may change the world."

A noted physicist corrects the popular delusion that all scientific laws are based on provable fact. He points out that not only is the uniformity of nature purely presumptive, but "the validity of similar basic scientific axioms is constantly being challenged—such as the no longer incontestable 'fact' that a straight line is the shortest distance between two points. In regard to spiritual healing," he continues, "let me say that another basic axiom is the assumption that matter can neither be created nor destroyed. Yet I have heard evidence that in more than one case of healing of the deaf, new eardrums have been instantly created. This may throw open to controversy the validity of this third axiom."

Nevertheless, the layman is still genuinely puzzled. What about the unchangeability of natural law, he wonders. Surely the known laws by which the universe is governed cannot be broken or suspended at the whim of a Creator, or for any other reason. The result would be inconceivable and universal chaos.

The physicist explains the difference between known law and the scientific axiom. There are certain indisputable laws, he tells us, such as the law of gravity, which are indeed unchangeable. On the other hand, an axiom is the *assumption* of truth, based on present knowledge. It serves as a starting point from which further research may proceed. But a scientific axiom is accepted as truth *only* until it is invalidated by the discovery of new evidence. Therefore, the competent scientist does not turn his back on evidence, however unlikely it may seem at first glance.

A physicist, who believes that physics will gradually be revolutionized as knowledge of spiritual healing increases, states: "The scientist cannot permit prejudice to blind him to fact. I have watched this healing power in action. I feel that on the basis of a few individual healings, one could validly claim 'wrong diagnosis,' or 'coincidence.' However, it is my opinion that the cumulative evidence rules out the 'wrong diagnosis' theory—while the frequent repetition of specific results cannot be ascribed by the honest scientist to mere 'coincidence.' There is here a definite implication of causative connection which warrants investigation.

Having studied much evidence relevant to miraculous healing, I must concede that an impressive number of healings are occurring as claimed."

How, then, do these physicists who accept non-medical healing as fact explain the phenomenon? They would appear to share unanimously the opinion of the physicist who cautiously states: "As these phenomena do not conform to any known law, I can only surmise that they are the manifestation of a higher law of which we are largely ignorant."

Some scientists whom I have interviewed term this unknown law a "spiritual" law—others do not—but the theory that there is in effect an as yet undiscovered "higher" law is gaining scientific acceptance.

The change of attitude of science toward religion is significantly reflected in the number of physicists who have turned to the Church for the ultimate answers to the universe which they had sought and not found in the scientific field. In checking the enrollment of several seminaries, I found that 40% of the student clergy hold degrees in science. "We're looking now for the *whole* answer," commented one of the erstwhile physicists. "We discovered some time ago that science alone can provide only fragments of the truth."

I have cited the high percentage of physicists entering the Church, not to imply that there is a general exodus from science to religion, which obviously is not true, nor would it be desirable. I have merely tried to point out that the concept of a higher law which transcends both physical and mental science has brought religion and science closer than they have ever been. No longer do the two appear hopelessly contradictory and irreconcilably incompatible; no longer does allegiance to the one cause necessitate negation of the other. We are slowly beginning to understand that they are interrelated and interdependent, with the final answers contingent on co-operation between the two.

I have not meant to give the impression that all scientists believe in God. Many do not. But my findings would seem to support the contention of Dr. Robert Millikan, Nobel prize winner physicist, who wrote me shortly before his death: "That there is an over-all plan of creation we can have no doubt. As Einstein and other great thinkers have said, there is a great intelligence manifested in all nature— and most competent scientists recognize the existence of a Supreme Being 'through whom we live and move and have our being.' "

A few avowed agnostics tend to feel that there is a purely scientific and materialistic justification for the so-called miracles. "When we learn more of the operation of the law which releases this healing energy," says one of these, "we will have a rational scientific explanation to offer. Yesterday, for example, it was inconceivable that the atom could be split. Today it is an accomplished fact. In the same manner, today's miracles of healing will be to-morrow's commonplaces."

Although the scientist is generally reluctant to concede the possibility that the healing miracles occurring today are due to the direct intervention of the Holy Spirit, those who hold this belief are not as far from the scientific viewpoint as might be supposed.

The thinking believer is fully aware of the danger of attributing an event not immediately explicable by current scientific knowledge to the direct intervention of God. He realizes that it is but a short step from faith into the quagmire of superstition. For this reason he is careful not to define a miracle as evidence of God's power to break or change His own laws. He claims, with the physicist, the existence of another law, a spiritual law to which his soul and mind and body are subject, a law which transcends, but does not violate, established scientific principle.

The believer concedes, with the scientist, that today's healing miracles may well be tomorrow's commonplaces. In man's ever-expanding knowledge, he sees the hand of God, steadily guiding and continually inspiring. But he who has known the healing power goes one step further. He has felt the hand of Christ upon his body, the grace of God upon his soul.

Unscientific, you think? So did I, until times without number I had witnessed the miracle of spiritual regeneration resulting from the power of redemptive love. This will forever defy scientific analysis.

Throughout the Gospels, Christ is revealed to us as the Saver of souls, the Healer of bodies. I asked myself an honest question: Am I presumptuous enough to decide arbitrarily that He retains the power to forgive sin, but has inexplicably lost the lesser power to heal bodies?

With my negative answer came the realization that for the Christian there will always be miracles. Man can never wholly comprehend the mind of God. His love cannot be mathematically computed, nor His compassion accurately measured in a test tube.

Through today's healing miracles, man is brought into a truer knowledge of his Saviour. This is the miracle which must transcend scientific explanation or achievement. But there is no conflict. Side by side, the believer in the healing power of the Holy Spirit, and the scientist seeking truth in an unknown law, strive to claim His promise: "I am come that they may have life and have it more abundantly."

19

The Keys of the Kingdom

THIS book was originally conceived as a report on the phenomenon of non-medical healings. It has ended as the story of an agnostic's journey into faith.

Let it be understood that I make no such obviously false claim as that healing is the only recognizable channel through which the Holy Spirit operates, or that it is the only road to true faith. I only say that for me and for many, it has proved the light which has shown the way. I see it as the Living Bread for which the Christian world has starved for so long.

The ministry of healing is a synthesis of the Church's other ministries and, in its own right, the most dynamic of them all. It is proving itself to be the great restorer, not only of the healing power, but of all spiritual power which the Church had virtually lost: a loss which has threatened to prostitute the living Christian faith into a mere system of Judeo-Christian philosophy.

A world hungry for God has, in self-defense, veiled its hunger with a mantle of indifference. Now, through the demonstrable evidence of God's healing power, this mantle is being replaced by the panoply of Christ, for any Christian who has witnessed His healing power cannot remain indifferent. For him, Christian hope becomes the complete assurance taught by our Lord, not the purely speculative thing it used to be. In compliance with His command to "follow thou Me," Christian faith becomes the heart's commitment to Jesus Christ—no longer solely the mind's belief of certain intellectually acceptable portions of the Gospel.

There are some who, for a long time to come, will steadfastly resist the idea of miracles. They will resolutely adhere to the philosophy described by Herbert Spencer as "the principle which is a bar against all information—which is proof against all arguments, and which cannot fail to keep a man in everlasting ignorance; that principle is contempt prior to investigation."

There are many who will continue to scoff at the miraculous because from childhood they have been taught to believe only half the Gospel. There are liberals who, like myself until only a short time ago, will deny the historicity of the New Testament miracles, not aware that in stripping His ministry of the miraculous, they are leaving it bereft of power.

Then there are the "modernists" who will concede the early miracles, but categorically reject His message of Good News—not aware, perhaps, that by their rejection they are robbing His ministry of purpose. To them, "Verily, verily, I say unto you, He that believeth on me, the works that I do shall he do also; and greater works than these shall he do" is not the vibrant promise charged with life which can transform the world; it is only a euphonious combination of mildly comforting words from John 14:12 —only half understood and not at all believed.

But what of those who with sincerity and truth say, "I have complete faith in God without direct evidence of His healing power"? These are the Christians of whom our Lord has said, "Blessed are they that have not seen, and yet have believed." These are the Christians of whom there are too few. Were they more numerous, the once flaming faith in the Saviour of mankind would not so largely have degenerated into lip service to a code of ethics.

But question these believers closely and you will find, as have I, that while they may not *need* the tangible evidence of the living God, they in no wise deny the Healing Christ who is our Redeemer. They are quick to recognize that His healing of sin and sickness, His redemption of the soul and deliverance of the body is the heart of the Gospel. His revelation of a wholly benevolent God, always accessible and of limitless power, is the crux of the message He came to give the world.

"And Jesus went about all the cities and villages, teaching in their synagogues, and preaching the gospel of the kingdom, and healing every sickness and every disease among the people" (Matt. 9:35).

Those of the faithful to whom spiritual healing is a new concept are quick to acknowledge the authority and indivisibility of His command: "Preach the Gospel and heal the sick." They sense a new cogency in His words: "All power is given unto me in heaven and in earth. Go ye therefore, and teach all nations ... whatsoever I have commanded you: and, lo, I am with you alway, even unto the end of the world" (Matt. 28: 18-20).

They have believed in their hearts that "Jesus Christ is the same yesterday, today, and forever," but until now, they have not seen these words translated into reality.

The Gospel records indicate that in all but one instance, our Lord's healings were instantaneous. This is not necessarily true today, when miraculous healings are often delayed. We must remember that the revival of spiritual healing is still in its infancy. We are in the process of a great spiritual awakening, but we have a long way to go before full spiritual consciousness.

In medicine there are certain physical factors which may inhibit the success of a simple operation. Hemorrhage may follow surgery, a blood clot may form, a bone may refuse to knit. Likewise in spiritual healing, there may be certain spiritual factors which temporarily hinder the inflow of the healing power of God. As sin separates us from God, it must obviously separate us from His healing power. Our souls, as the channels for His grace, are sometimes blocked by unrecognized sin, as in the typical case of a woman suffering from pre-malignant leucoplacia (thickening of the vocal cords).

Following surgery, her condition worsened and became so precarious that the doctors warned her family that recovery was doubtful. The patient then attended her first healing service, which resulted in immediate and dramatic improvement in her condition. For three weeks improvement continued and then stopped as suddenly as it had begun. Convinced that God willed her healing, the woman continued to receive the healing Sacraments, at the same time probing her soul for the cause of her relapse. Her final realization that she was harboring a feeling of deep resentment against an individual who had once done her an injustice proved the key. Through prayer, she overcame her resentment. Unobstructed, now, the healing power of the Holy Spirit poured into her body. She is today in perfect health.

"But what happens to a person's faith if he is not healed —as some are not?" is a common question, asked most frequently perhaps by those many clergymen who would like to institute a healing ministry, but are admittedly afraid of failure.

Theoretically, the fear that if an individual fails to receive a physical healing he will turn from God is justified. Practically, as experience proves, it just doesn't work that way. As the Rev. Richard Spread notes: "No matter what the theorists may say, spiritual healing is essentially spiritual in character ... This accounts for the fact that those who do not receive physical healing do not lose their faith in God. They *always* receive spiritual grace ... The spiritual power received is wonderful and obvious to all who come in contact with that person." This statement is confirmed by everyone who administers spiritual healing, and I have personally seen its truth demonstrated. The faithful who have not been cured of their bodily ailments have received healings of the spirit which transcend in wonder even the most dramatic physical healings.

For the benefit of those who worry over what will happen if an individual is not physically healed, let me state that just as anyone undergoing a simple appendectomy has every reason to suppose that he will recover, so has anyone seeking divine healing every reason to suppose that he will be completely healed through the power of God.

Those who fear failure must accept the well-proved truth: there are no failures in spiritual healing. No one who has felt the healing power, whether or not he has been physically healed, remains spiritually unchanged. He is the recipient of unseen but none the less positive stigmata, the marks of which he will carry always on his soul. He has received an inpouring of spiritual grace which, in turning him to the Lord in faith, gratitude, and service, has transformed his life.

"Seek ye *first* the kingdom of God" (Matt. 6:33). The healing ministry never lets us forget that "the important thing is not the healing of the body, but the soul's salvation." Only now have I completely understood and thoroughly believed these words. I began this book with utter amazement at the physical healings I had witnessed. I conclude it filled with a far greater wonder at the spiritual fruits I have seen ripen before my eyes. It is abundantly clear that our Lord's emphasis was not on healing as such. He did not come to be a doctor, He came to bring us God. But He showed us how inextricably woven together are the healing of the spirit and the curing of the body. "If I with the finger of God cast out devils, no doubt the kingdom of God is upon you" (Luke 11:20). "Heal the sick . . ." He said, "and say unto them, The kingdom of God is come nigh unto you" (Luke 10:9).

I have seen the sick healed, and I have glimpsed, through them, the Kingdom.

I have seen in the healing Church the same transforming power of the Apostles, who knew they were handling the power of God.

I have seen in the believing laity the fervor of the early Christians who, certain of the fulfilment of our Lord's promises, were reborn into joy.

I have seen the spiritual impact of the revitalized healing ministry on thousands of people, as they watch the healing clergy go forth as did the Apostles: "They preached every where, the Lord working with them, and confirming the word with signs following" (Mark 16:20).

I now stand convinced that the present world-wide revelation of the healing power of God has placed in our hands the Keys of the Kingdom. What we do with them must be the Christian world's own decision. We can throw them to the ground, as did they who crucified Christ—or we can use them to fling wide the gates of Heaven.

SOME BOOKS FOR FURTHER READING

A Doctor Heals by Faith, Christopher Woodard. Max Parrish, London, 1953.

The Healing Light, Agnes Sanford. Macalester Park, 1947.

**The Voyage to Lourdes,* Alexis Carrel. Harper and Brothers, 1950.

**Recovery,* Starr Dailey. Macalester Park, 1948.

Everyman's Search, Rebecca Beard. Harper and Brothers, 1950.

**Stretching Forth Thine Hand To Heal,* R. A. H. Spread. Morehouse-Barlow, 1937.

Psychology, Religion, and Healing, Leslie D. Weatherhead. Abingdon, 1951.

Christian Healing, Evelyn Frost. A. R. Mowbray, 1940.

**Divine Antidote to Sin, Sickness and Death,* Frank Riale The Christian Work, 1921.

**The Living Touch,* Dorothy Kerin. G. Bell and Sons, Ltd., 1914.

**The Church and Healing,* Carl J. Scherzer. Westminster, 1950.

Abundant Living, E. Stanley Jones. Abingdon, 1942.

**Health and Salvation,* Wallace E. Conkling. Morehouse-Barlow, 1952.

**Manual of Christian Healing,* John G. Banks. St. Luke's Press, 1953.

**You Can Be Healed,* Clifton E. and Clinto J. Kew. Prentice-Hall, 1953.

New Concepts of Healing, A. Graham Ikin. Hodder and Stoughton, 1955.

He Heals Today, Elsie Salmon. Arthur James, Evesham, England, 1951.

You Can Be Healed, Clara Palmer. Unity.

Let Go and Let God, A. E. Cliffe. Prentice-Hall, 1951.

* Out of print, but may be available in libraries.

191

Sharing, An International Journal of Christian Healing, published monthly. Ed., Ethel Tulloch Banks, 2243 Front St., San Diego, Calif.

Pamphlets
Religion and Health, Alfred Price. St. Stephen's Church, Philadelphia 7, Pa.
Answering Prayers, Louise Eggleston. World Literature Prayer Group, Ghent Methodist Church, Norfolk 7, Va.
Healing, Alfred Price. St. Stephen's Church, Philadelphia 7, Pa.
Fundamentals of the Ministry of Healing, J. A. C. Murray. Guild of Health, London.
Tracts by Ethel T. and John G. Banks. St. Luke's Press, 2243 Front St., San Diego, Calif.

OTHER BOOKS BY THE SAME AUTHOR

IN THE MIDST OF LIFE

WHERE THERE'S SMOKE
The Mystery of Christian Healing

MOREHOUSE-BARLOW CO.
14 EAST 41ST STREET
NEW YORK, NEW YORK 10017